First published in 2024 by Hungry Tomato Ltd
F15, Old Bakery Studios, Blewetts Wharf,
Malpas Road, Truro, Cornwall, TR1 1QH, UK.

Thanks to our creative team:
Senior Graphic Designer: Amy Harvey
Editor: Millie Burdett
Editor: Holly Thornton

A CIP catalog record for this book is available from the British Library.

ISBN: 9781912108565

Printed and bound in China

Discover more at
www.hungrytomato.com
www.mybeetlebooks.com

CATS

An illustrated guide to cool cats!

By Eliza Jeffery

Illustrated by Marina Halak

CONTENTS

Super Shorthair Cats

Lovable Longhair Cats

Funky Feline Features

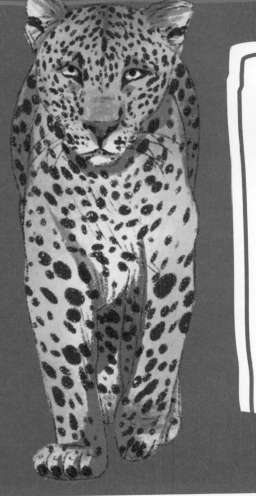

Cunning Wild Cats

Words in **bold** can be found in the glossary.

THE WORLD OF CATS

Get ready to explore the wonderful world of cats! From the tiny Singapura to the big, wild tiger, there are so many different types of cats to discover.

WHAT IS A SPECIES?

A species is a group of living things, like animals or plants, that share **unique** characteristics. For example, tigers and **domestic** cats are two different species. There are around 40 cat species in total, some of which can be separated into smaller groups called breeds.

Big or small, they've got it all!

A chausie cat and a mountain lion, but which one is which?

WHERE DO CATS COME FROM?

All cats are **descendants** of the African wildcat, a species believed to have emerged 12 million years ago! This cat is still around today, alongside many other types of wild cat. There are plenty of new species that have been domesticated by humans too – these are the types of cats that we keep as pets!

WHAT IS A BREED?

A breed is a small group of animals within a species that all share the same (or very similar) appearance and characteristics, making them easy to identify. There are lots of different breeds, and they can vary wildly in size, shape, hairiness and personality.

Not all cats belong to a specific breed. Some cats are a mixture of lots of different breeds. They can make fantastic and unique pets, and can often be found looking for a loving home at rescue or **rehoming shelters.**

They all have great personalities and talents!

GETTING A CAT?

Maybe you already have a cat in your family, or maybe you'd like to in the future. Owning a cat can be fun and rewarding, but it's also a big responsibility. Some cats need a lot of grooming, care and attention. Before buying or adopting a cat, you should always carefully research their breed and think about whether you are able to give them everything they need to be happy.

Some cats love to get up to mischief!

TAKING CARE OF CATS

When it comes to taking care of a cat, there is a lot to consider! Some cats need a lot more looking after than others. Here are a few areas to consider when you are looking into what your cat needs to be happy.

GROOMING

Grooming is a very important part of owning a cat. Some cats require a brush once a week, whereas some require brushing every day! The length of your cat's coat will affect how much attention it requires.

DIFFERENT COATS

Although most cats have a single coat of fur, some have two coats (double coat), and a handful even have three coats (triple coat)! Make sure you do your research on your cat breed to ensure the best grooming routine.

Some cats, such as the Turkish Angora, have single coats which gives them silky, smooth and fine fur.

Cats such as Persians have double coats, which means they have an added extra layer of warmth and their hair is usually thicker.

Cats like the Siberian have triple coats which means they have extra layers of fur to help withstand cold weather.

KEEPING CLEAN & HEALTHY

Cats naturally groom and keep themselves clean, but they need some help from their owners too! This includes cleaning their ears, brushing their teeth, clipping their nails and even washing them. You may have to be patient with your pet when it comes to these tasks, but they are very important in keeping your pet healthy.

Cats such as the Savannah and the Turkish Van can often be found playing with water and love bath time.

Bath time is fun for some but not all cats enjoy it!

Cats love scratching posts, climbing and toys. A ball of string will keep them entertained for ages!

EXERCISE & PLAY

Regardless of whether your cat lives indoors or is allowed to explore the world outside, exercise is important for keeping your cat happy. And the best way for your pet to exercise is through play! You might want to get involved with playtime too! This is a perfect way to bond with your cat and make sure it is staying active.

SUPER SHORTHAIR CATS

Most cat species have developed short hair over time, including wild and domesticated breeds. This allows them to move and hunt easily, as well as keep them cool in warmer months.

The first cats to be domesticated are believed to have had a short coat of fur. When it comes to looking after domestic cats, the shorthair breeds are easy for owners to maintain, often only needing to be groomed once a week. Let's delve into the world of super shorthair cats!

Abyssinian

This wild-looking cat is believed to have descended from Ethiopia and been taken to the United Kingdom by soldiers in the 1860s. Abyssinians have a lean, muscular build and are extremely intelligent. They are playful creatures and make wonderful companions.

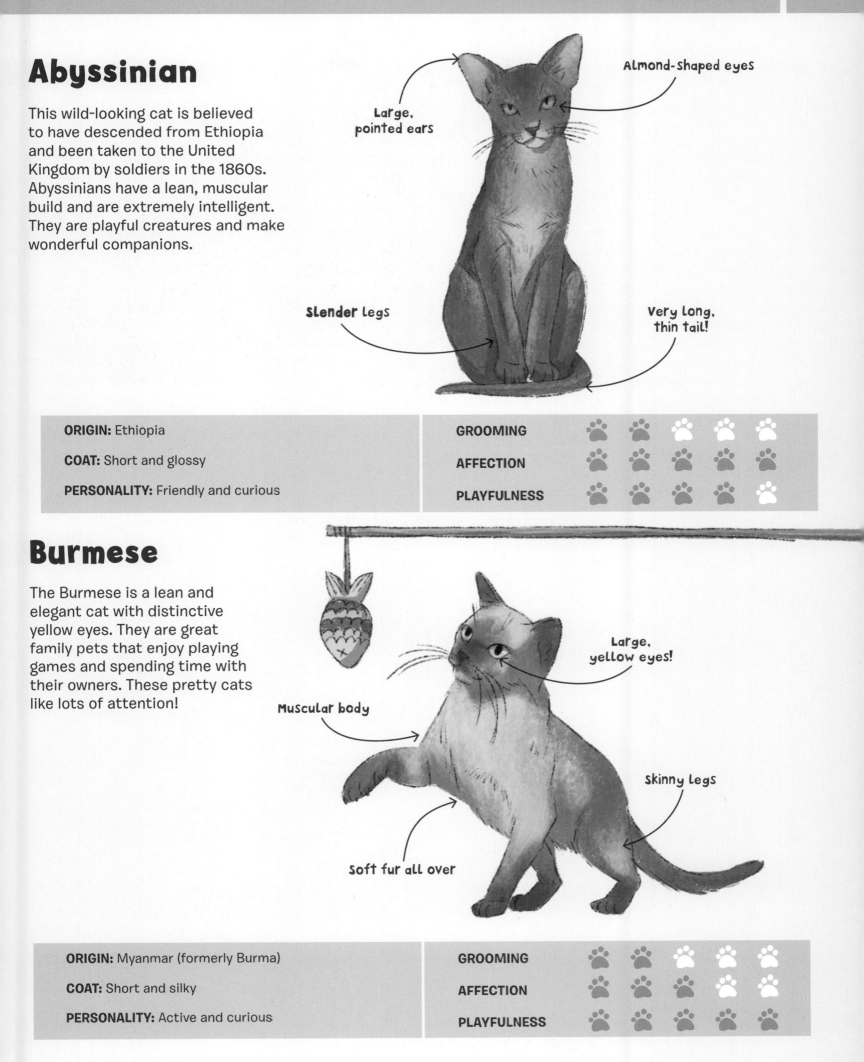

Large, pointed ears

Almond-shaped eyes

Slender legs

Very long, thin tail!

ORIGIN: Ethiopia

COAT: Short and glossy

PERSONALITY: Friendly and curious

GROOMING

AFFECTION

PLAYFULNESS

Burmese

The Burmese is a lean and elegant cat with distinctive yellow eyes. They are great family pets that enjoy playing games and spending time with their owners. These pretty cats like lots of attention!

Muscular body

Large, yellow eyes!

Skinny legs

Soft fur all over

ORIGIN: Myanmar (formerly Burma)

COAT: Short and silky

PERSONALITY: Active and curious

GROOMING

AFFECTION

PLAYFULNESS

Havana

The Havana is a rare breed, easy to spot thanks to their brown fur and bright, green eyes. They are very intelligent creatures that can be trained to play fetch! These felines are very sociable, so they don't like to be left alone for long periods of time.

Bright, green eyes!

Fur can be chocolatey-brown to almost black!

Thin, strong body

ORIGIN: USA

COAT: Short and smooth

PERSONALITY: Playful and gentle

GROOMING

AFFECTION

PLAYFULNESS

Korat

The Korat is considered a good luck charm in Thailand. This pretty feline's coat is always a silvery-blue, making its green eyes stand out! This sociable cat enjoys lots of interactive play and is very loving toward its owners.

Heart-shaped nose

They are believed to bring lots of good luck!

Muscular body

ORIGIN: Thailand

COAT: Short and shimmery

PERSONALITY: Affectionate and friendly

GROOMING

AFFECTION

PLAYFULNESS

Chartreux

Chartreux are best known for their dark silver fur and round, golden eyes. They have a sturdy build, with a muscular body and strong legs. Chartreux are calm and quiet cats that appreciate lots of attention in the home. Even though these felines do enjoy playtime, they would much prefer to take a nap!

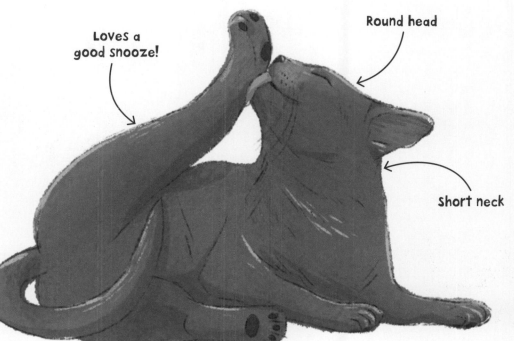

Loves a good snooze!

Round head

Short neck

	GROOMING	🐾 🐾 🐾 🐾 🐾
ORIGIN: France	AFFECTION	🐾 🐾 🐾 🐾 🐾
COAT: Thick and woolly	PLAYFULNESS	🐾 🐾 🐾 🐾 🐾
PERSONALITY: Quiet and curious		

Bombay

This panther look-alike has a jet-black coat and gold, round eyes. These friendly felines are often found in warm, comfy spots around the house. The Bombay cat is very sociable and active with its owners.

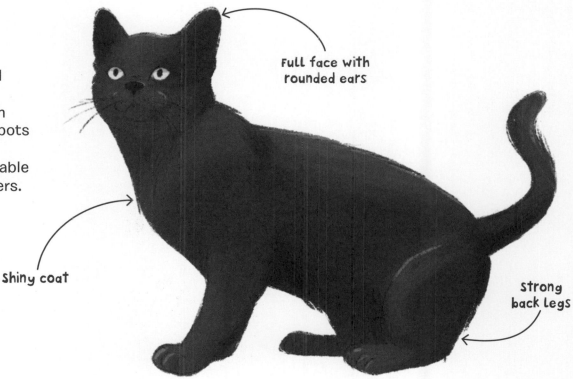

Full face with rounded ears

Shiny coat

Strong back legs

	GROOMING	🐾 🐾 🐾 🐾 🐾
ORIGIN: USA	AFFECTION	🐾 🐾 🐾 🐾 🐾
COAT: Short and glossy	PLAYFULNESS	🐾 🐾 🐾 🐾 🐾
PERSONALITY: Mischievous and outgoing		

Toyger

Nicknamed the "toy tiger", this breed of cat looks like a small version of a tiger (page 50)! Despite looking like a wild cat, the toyger was bred to be sociable and friendly toward its owners and other household pets.

Brown-striped tabby coat

Distinctive face markings

Powerful legs

ORIGIN: USA		GROOMING	🐾 🐾 🐾 🐾 🐾
COAT: Short and dense		AFFECTION	🐾 🐾 🐾 🐾 🐾
PERSONALITY: Laid-back and friendly		PLAYFULNESS	🐾 🐾 🐾 🐾 🐾

Savannah

The Savannah is best known for its dog-like personality. Unlike many cats, this striking feline enjoys playing in water and loves to play fetch! This breed came from mixing a domestic cat with a wild serval (page 56), giving the Savannah its interesting coat pattern.

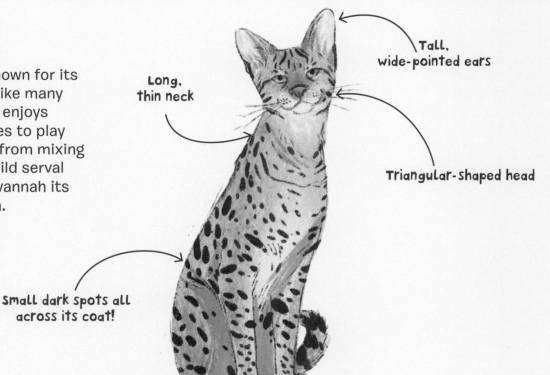

Tall, wide-pointed ears

Long, thin neck

Triangular-shaped head

Small dark spots all across its coat!

ORIGIN: USA		GROOMING	🐾 🐾 🐾 🐾 🐾
COAT: Short and dense		AFFECTION	🐾 🐾 🐾 🐾 🐾
PERSONALITY: Adventurous and loyal		PLAYFULNESS	🐾 🐾 🐾 🐾 🐾

Bengal

This striking feline is just as energetic and independent as its wild cat look-alike! Bengal cats have high energy levels, which means they are lots of fun to play with but can also be a handful for their owners!

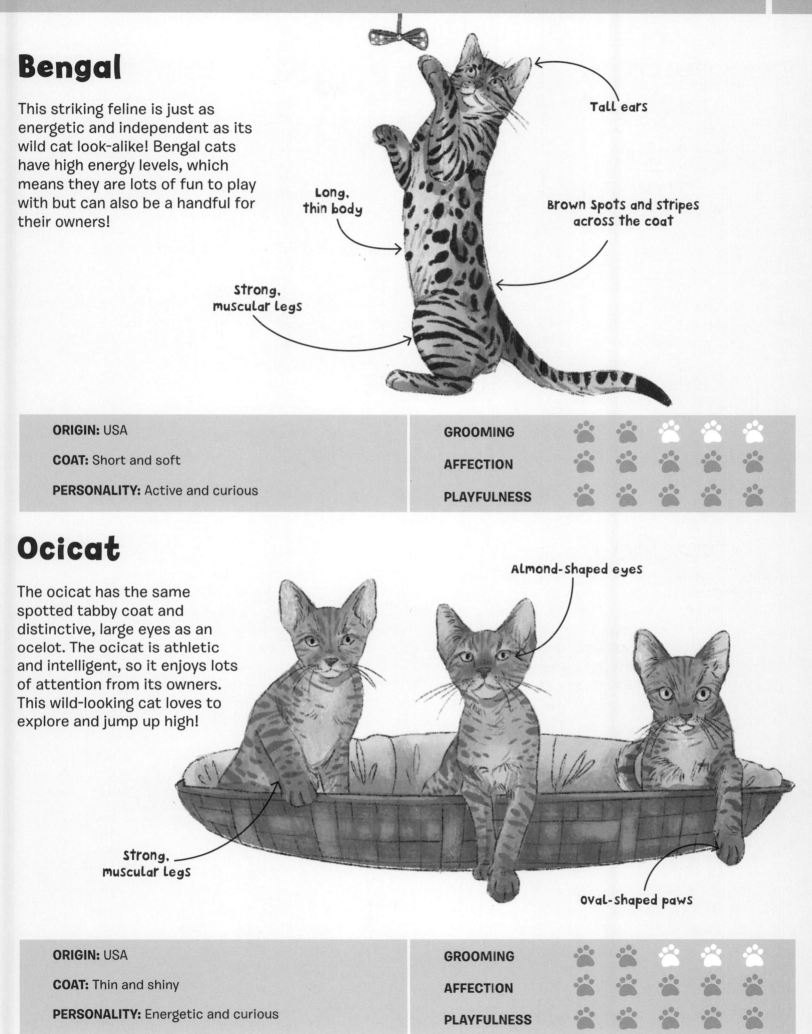

Tall ears

Long, thin body

Brown spots and stripes across the coat

strong, muscular legs

ORIGIN: USA

COAT: Short and soft

PERSONALITY: Active and curious

GROOMING

AFFECTION

PLAYFULNESS

Ocicat

The ocicat has the same spotted tabby coat and distinctive, large eyes as an ocelot. The ocicat is athletic and intelligent, so it enjoys lots of attention from its owners. This wild-looking cat loves to explore and jump up high!

Almond-shaped eyes

strong, muscular legs

Oval-shaped paws

ORIGIN: USA

COAT: Thin and shiny

PERSONALITY: Energetic and curious

GROOMING

AFFECTION

PLAYFULNESS

Snowshoe

The snowshoe is easy to spot by its bright blue eyes and distinctive mix of light and dark fur. Very playful and sociable, this sweet feline relies greatly on its owners, so it doesn't enjoy being left alone for too long!

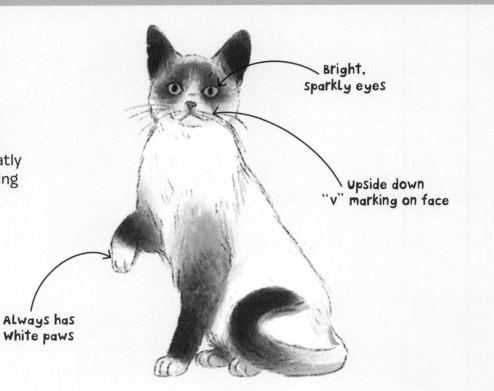

Bright, sparkly eyes

Upside down "v" marking on face

Always has white paws

ORIGIN: USA	**GROOMING**	🐾 🐾 🐾 🐾 🐾
COAT: Short and thick	**AFFECTION**	🐾 🐾 🐾 🐾 🐾
PERSONALITY: Sociable and affectionate	**PLAYFULNESS**	🐾 🐾 🐾 🐾 🐾

Long tail helps with balance

Loves to play with toys, like balls and feather wands!

Australian Mist

The Australian Mist was the first domestic cat to be bred in Australia. Its coat has a soft, shadowy appearance, which gives it its misty name. This friendly feline is a mix between an Abyssinian (page 13) and Burmese cat (page 13).

Wide ears that tilt forward

Long, thick tail

can be cheeky and mischevious!

ORIGIN: Australia	**GROOMING** 🐾🐾🐾🐾🐾
COAT: Tough and glossy	**AFFECTION** 🐾🐾🐾🐾🐾
PERSONALITY: Friendly and mellow	**PLAYFULNESS** 🐾🐾🐾🐾🐾

Sokoke

The Sokoke is a very rare breed of domesticated cat. These elegant felines make close family bonds and are known for communicating with their owners by meowing lots! They are considered one of the smartest cats in the world, and love to play.

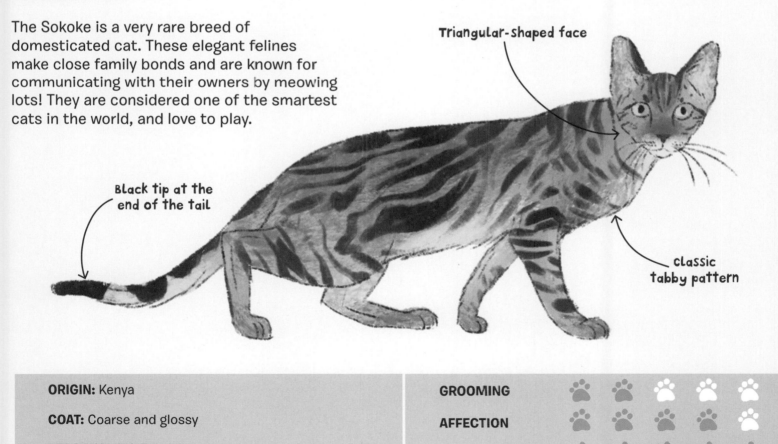

Triangular-shaped face

Black tip at the end of the tail

classic tabby pattern

ORIGIN: Kenya	**GROOMING** 🐾🐾🐾🐾🐾
COAT: Coarse and glossy	**AFFECTION** 🐾🐾🐾🐾🐾
PERSONALITY: Friendly and curious	**PLAYFULNESS** 🐾🐾🐾🐾🐾

Exotic Shorthair

This cat has a very expressive face, and spends most of the time looking very grumpy! The Exotic shorthair can be very affectionate and loyal toward its owners, but not so much strangers. It likes playing but enjoy cuddles on the sofa just as much!

Large, round eyes

Flat face

Bushy tail

ORIGIN: USA		
COAT: Soft and thick		
PERSONALITY: Friendly and calm		

GROOMING	🐾🐾🐾
AFFECTION	🐾🐾
PLAYFULNESS	🐾🐾🐾

Oriental

The Oriental is a breed of domestic cat that has been developed from the Siamese cat (page 42). Their coats range from the brightest white to the darkest black. They are known for having large, wide-stretching ears! This slender feline enjoys being around its owners and has lots of energy for them too.

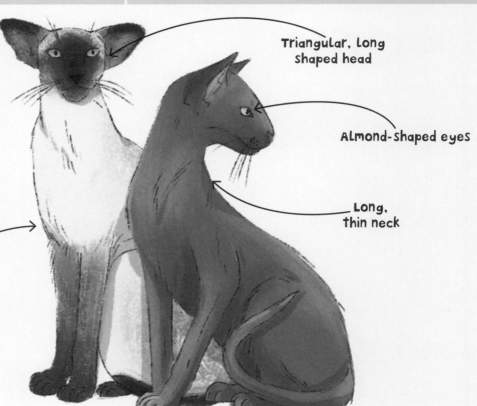

Triangular, long shaped head

Almond-shaped eyes

Long, thin neck

Keeps its owners busy and on their toes!

ORIGIN: United Kingdom		
COAT: Thin and glossy		
PERSONALITY: Lively and intelligent		

GROOMING	🐾🐾
AFFECTION	🐾🐾🐾🐾🐾
PLAYFULNESS	🐾🐾🐾🐾🐾

Seychellois

Seychellois are elegant and slender cats. Similarly to oriental cats (page 20), they are known for their large, wide ears and long triangular faces. These active cats are very vocal and want their owners' attention at all times!

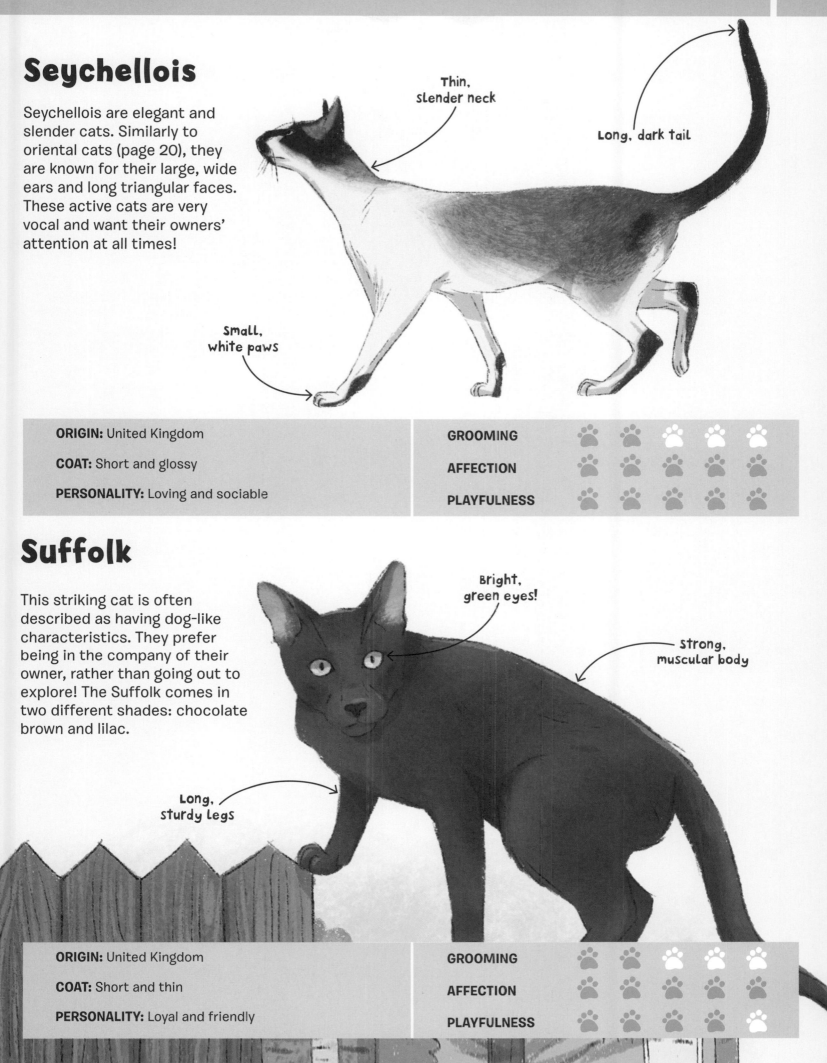

Thin, slender neck

Long, dark tail

Small, white paws

ORIGIN: United Kingdom

COAT: Short and glossy

PERSONALITY: Loving and sociable

GROOMING

AFFECTION

PLAYFULNESS

Suffolk

This striking cat is often described as having dog-like characteristics. They prefer being in the company of their owner, rather than going out to explore! The Suffolk comes in two different shades: chocolate brown and lilac.

Bright, green eyes!

Strong, muscular body

Long, sturdy legs

ORIGIN: United Kingdom

COAT: Short and thin

PERSONALITY: Loyal and friendly

GROOMING

AFFECTION

PLAYFULNESS

American Shorthair

Despite its name, the American shorthair descended from working cats from Europe. They were taken over to the USA in the 1600s, after being used on boats to protect cargo from rodents. Now popular pets, these cats are playful, curious, and still love to hunt!

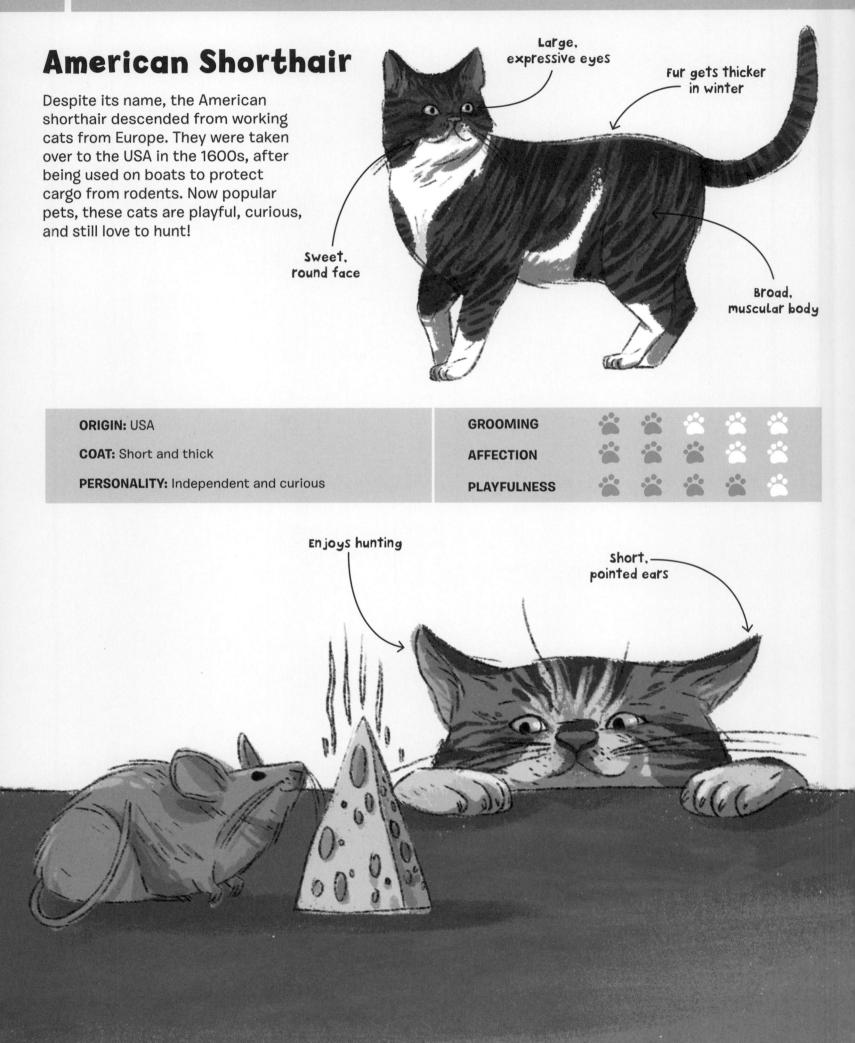

Large, expressive eyes

Fur gets thicker in winter

Sweet, round face

Broad, muscular body

ORIGIN: USA

COAT: Short and thick

PERSONALITY: Independent and curious

GROOMING

AFFECTION

PLAYFULNESS

Enjoys hunting

Short, pointed ears

British Shorthair

This cute companion is one of the oldest breeds in the United Kingdom. Although sometimes called British Blues after their lovely silver-blue coat, they can also be cream or tabby. Calm and well-behaved, they make perfect pets.

Short, thick neck

chubby cheeks

strong legs

Firm, round paws

ORIGIN: United Kingdom

COAT: Short and thick

PERSONALITY: Loyal and laid-back

GROOMING

AFFECTION

PLAYFULNESS

Chinese Li Hua

Also known as Dragon Li, this breed is thought to have descended from wildcats centuries ago! Considered one of the earliest domestic cats, this fine feline is good with families and pets, and is easy to care for.

Weekly brushing keeps coat shiny

Brown mackerel tabby coat

Bright, almond-shaped eyes

Black-tipped tail

ORIGIN: China

COAT: Short and smooth

PERSONALITY: Intelligent and friendly

GROOMING

AFFECTION

PLAYFULNESS

LOVABLE LONGHAIR CATS

It is believed that domestic cats only began to develop long hair due to **crossbreeding**. These felines have beautiful coats but require a lot of upkeep from their owners!

Longhair cats often shed their fur, especially during warmer months, and most require grooming every day to keep their coats soft and luxurious. Let's explore the world of lovable longhair cats!

Persian

The Persian cat is extremely popular among cat owners. This glamorous feline is known for its friendly personality, flat face, and thick, silky coat. This is one of the oldest cat breeds, dating all the way back to the 1600s.

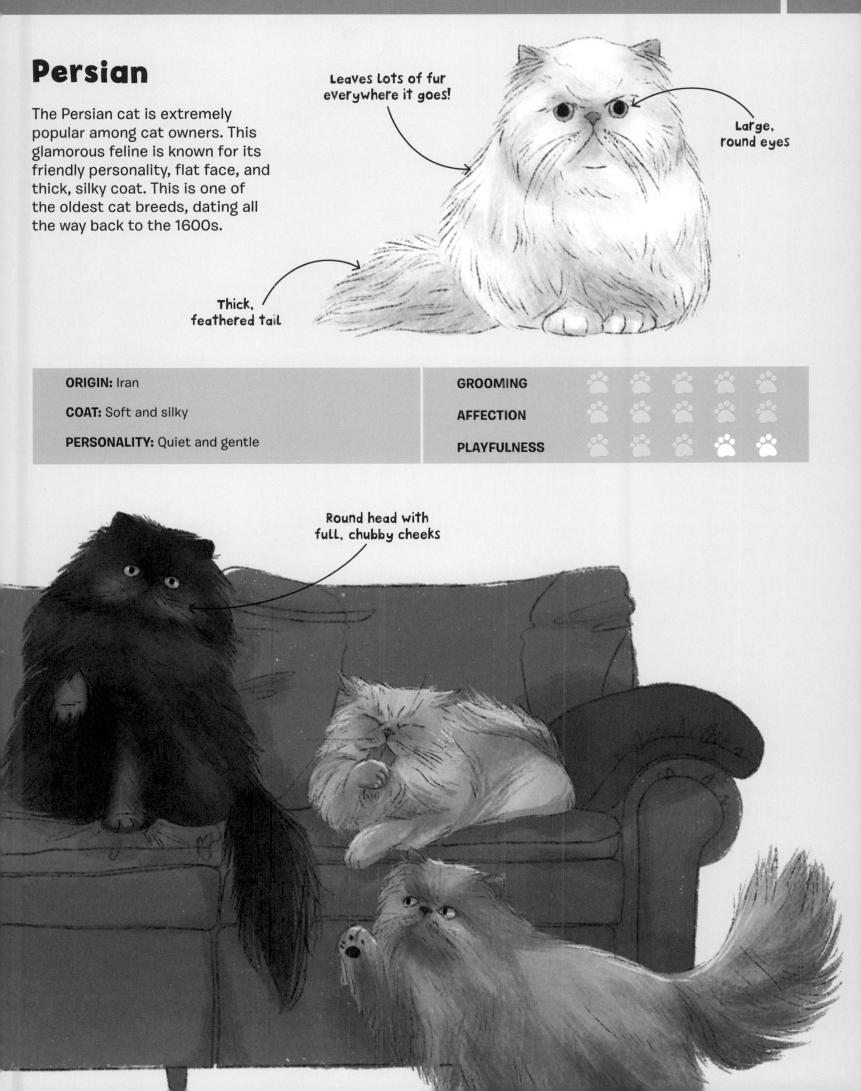

Leaves lots of fur everywhere it goes!

Large, round eyes

Thick, feathered tail

ORIGIN: Iran

COAT: Soft and silky

PERSONALITY: Quiet and gentle

GROOMING

AFFECTION

PLAYFULNESS

Round head with full, chubby cheeks

Birman

This beautiful feline is best known for its bright, blue eyes and thick, soft coat. The Birman loves to be around its owners and can be needy at times, meowing when it would like more attention!

Piercing, round eyes

Full cheeks

White paws like gloves!

ORIGIN: Myanmar (formerly Burma)	**GROOMING** 🐾🐾🐾🐾🐾
COAT: Soft and silky	**AFFECTION** 🐾🐾🐾🐾🐾
PERSONALITY: Affectionate and clingy	**PLAYFULNESS** 🐾🐾🐾🐾🐾

Kurilian Bobtail

The Kurilian bobtail is often described as having a tail similar to a rabbit's! This striking cat has a short but fluffy tail and wild-looking coat. They are very clever, love to play and can be taught tricks.

Bright, gold/amber eyes

Large body

Loves learning new things!

ORIGIN: Kuril Islands	**GROOMING** 🐾🐾🐾🐾🐾
COAT: Soft and silky	**AFFECTION** 🐾🐾🐾🐾🐾
PERSONALITY: Sociable and intelligent	**PLAYFULNESS** 🐾🐾🐾🐾🐾

Minuet (Napoleon)

Named after the French conqueror Napoleon Bonaparte for its short legs and big personality, this charming cat is a fairly new breed, created by mixing a Munchkin (page 42) with a Persian (page 25) in the 1990s. The Minuet is sometimes referred to as the "dachshund" of the cat world!

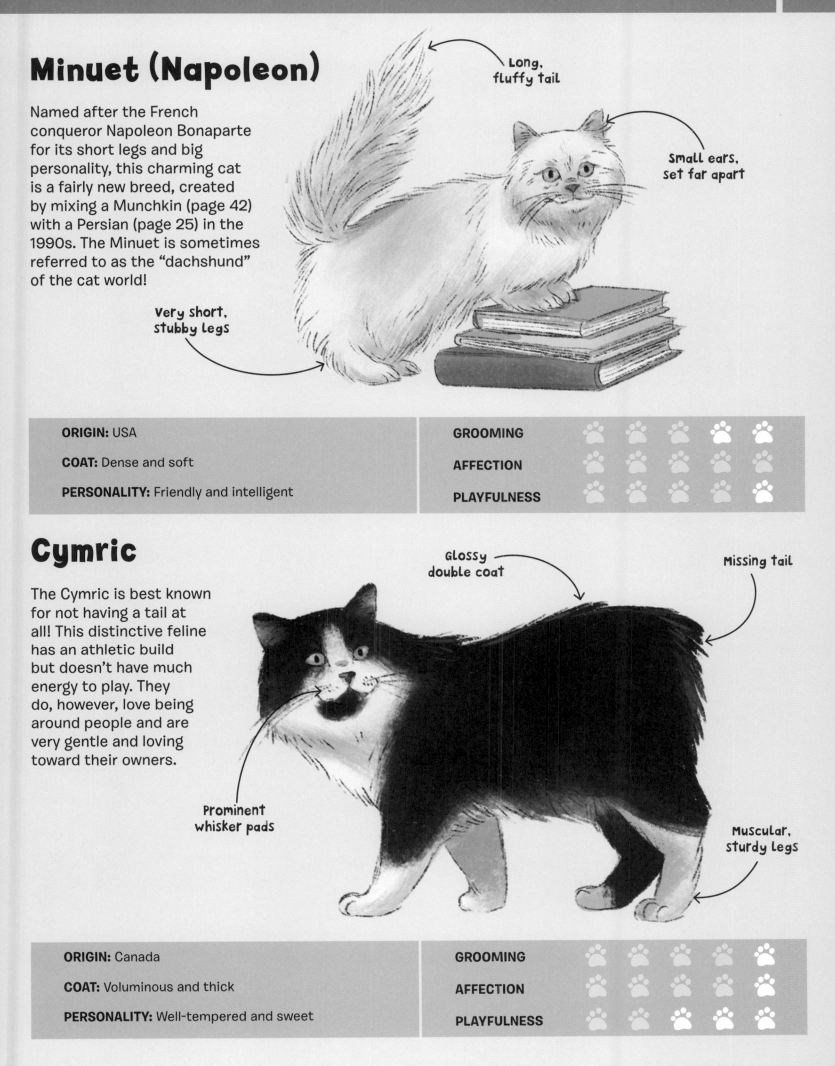

Long, fluffy tail

Small ears, set far apart

Very short, stubby legs

ORIGIN: USA

COAT: Dense and soft

PERSONALITY: Friendly and intelligent

GROOMING

AFFECTION

PLAYFULNESS

Cymric

The Cymric is best known for not having a tail at all! This distinctive feline has an athletic build but doesn't have much energy to play. They do, however, love being around people and are very gentle and loving toward their owners.

Glossy double coat

Missing tail

Prominent whisker pads

Muscular, sturdy legs

ORIGIN: Canada

COAT: Voluminous and thick

PERSONALITY: Well-tempered and sweet

GROOMING

AFFECTION

PLAYFULNESS

Ragamuffin

Ragamuffins are a large breed of cat that came from a new development of the ragdoll (below). These relaxed felines are known for being gentle and patient around children. Although they do enjoy playing, they would much prefer a cuddle!

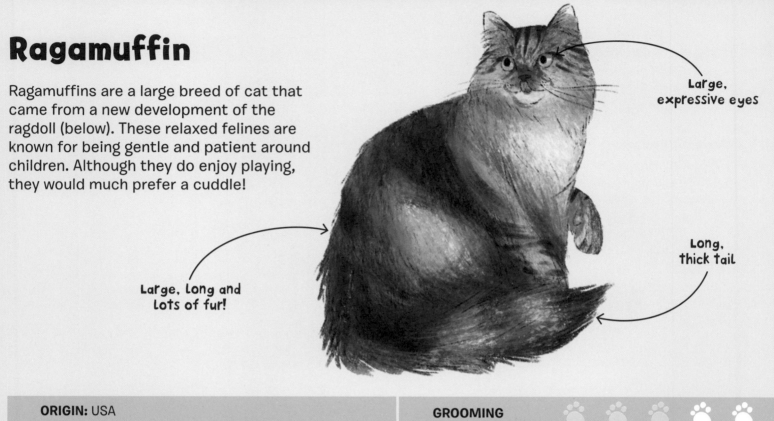

Large, expressive eyes

Long, thick tail

Large, Long and lots of fur!

ORIGIN: USA	**GROOMING**
COAT: Silky and soft	**AFFECTION**
PERSONALITY: Loyal and laid-back	**PLAYFULNESS**

Ragdoll

The ragdoll is a popular breed among families due to its playfulness, calm nature and friendly expressions. This well-built feline is intelligent and eager to please, spending most of its time following its owners around.

Wide, pointy ears

Bright, blue eyes

Who wouldn't want to give me a cuddle?

Shorter fur on legs

ORIGIN: USA	**GROOMING**
COAT: Soft and silky	**AFFECTION**
PERSONALITY: Peaceful and sweet	**PLAYFULNESS**

British Longhair

British longhair cats have attractive long, flowing coats. These round-faced felines are known for their sweet nature and loyalty to their owners. They are playful as kittens but take on a lazier approach to life as they get older!

Round, golden eyes

Prominent whisker pads

Brush-like tail

		GROOMING	🐾 🐾 🐾 🐾 🐾
ORIGIN: United Kingdom		AFFECTION	🐾 🐾 🐾 🐾 🐾
COAT: Thick and soft		PLAYFULNESS	🐾 🐾 🐾 🐾 🐾
PERSONALITY: Calm and friendly			

Siberian

The Siberian is an ancient breed from Russia, known for its triple coated fur that helps it stay warm in cold weather. This beautiful feline is very affectionate and enjoys the company of humans, as well as other animals. These large cats take five years to reach full size.

Pink nose

This cat has a very fluffy coat!

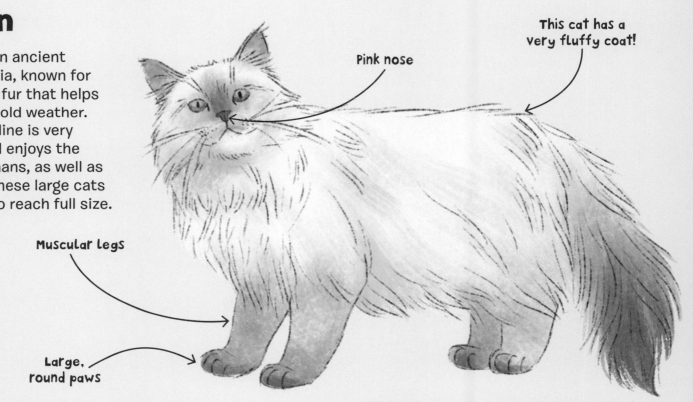

Muscular legs

Large, round paws

		GROOMING	🐾 🐾 🐾 🐾 🐾
ORIGIN: Russia		AFFECTION	🐾 🐾 🐾 🐾 🐾
COAT: Water-resistant and soft		PLAYFULNESS	🐾 🐾 🐾 🐾 🐾
PERSONALITY: Friendly and patient			

Norwegian Forest

Norwegian forest cats are large cats, known for their beautiful silvery fur. Their dense, double coat keeps them warm, becoming even thicker during winter months. These majestic felines love to explore!

Bright green eyes!

White markings on chest

Likes to play outdoors, whatever the weather!

ORIGIN: United Kingdom	GROOMING	🐾 🐾 🐾 🐾 🐾
COAT: Short and thick	AFFECTION	🐾 🐾 🐾 🐾 🐾
PERSONALITY: Loyal and laid-back	PLAYFULNESS	🐾 🐾 🐾 🐾

Selkirk Rex

With thick, untamed curls, the Selkirk Rex instantly stands out from other breeds. This unusual-coated feline is known for being extremely affectionate, spending most of its time following its owners around. It loves cuddles as much as it loves to play games!

They even have curly whiskers!

Thick, white hair surrounds the neck

Large, round paws

ORIGIN: USA	GROOMING	🐾 🐾 🐾 🐾 🐾
COAT: Thick and curly	AFFECTION	🐾 🐾 🐾 🐾 🐾
PERSONALITY: Gentle and sociable	PLAYFULNESS	🐾 🐾 🐾 🐾 🐾

Somali

You can spot a Somali cat because of its large, fox-like tail. This endearing feline is a longhair version of the Abyssinian (page 13), sharing its striking features and bundles of energy. This cat is known for its impressive jumping and climbing skills!

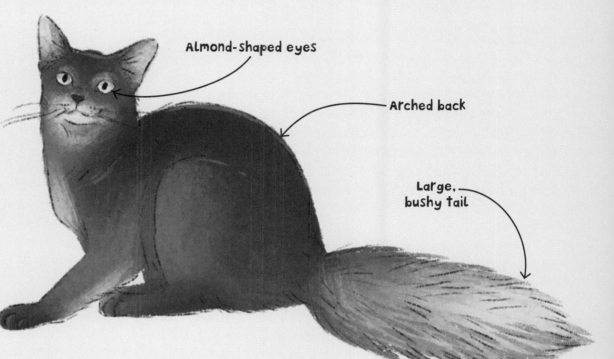

Almond-shaped eyes

Arched back

Large, bushy tail

ORIGIN: USA	**GROOMING**	🐾 🐾 🐾 🐾 🐾
COAT: Fine and soft	**AFFECTION**	🐾 🐾 🐾 🐾 🐾
PERSONALITY: Energetic and curious	**PLAYFULNESS**	🐾 🐾 🐾 🐾 🐾

LaPerm

Similar to the Selkirk Rex (page 30), the LaPerm has a coat of soft wavy fur and tight curls. They love the company of humans and are known for purring loudly to show they are happy. Charming and sociable, LaPerms are also very active and enjoy playing fetch!

Large, rounded ears

Almond-shaped eyes

Tightest curls around the chest

ORIGIN: USA	**GROOMING**	🐾 🐾 🐾 🐾 🐾
COAT: Curly and soft	**AFFECTION**	🐾 🐾 🐾 🐾 🐾
PERSONALITY: Intelligent and people-loving	**PLAYFULNESS**	🐾 🐾 🐾 🐾 🐾

Javanese

Javanese cats are always on the move! Agile and brave, they are often found climbing tall trees, or finding high perches to reach. They are also very vocal cats, happy to let their owners know when they want their food!

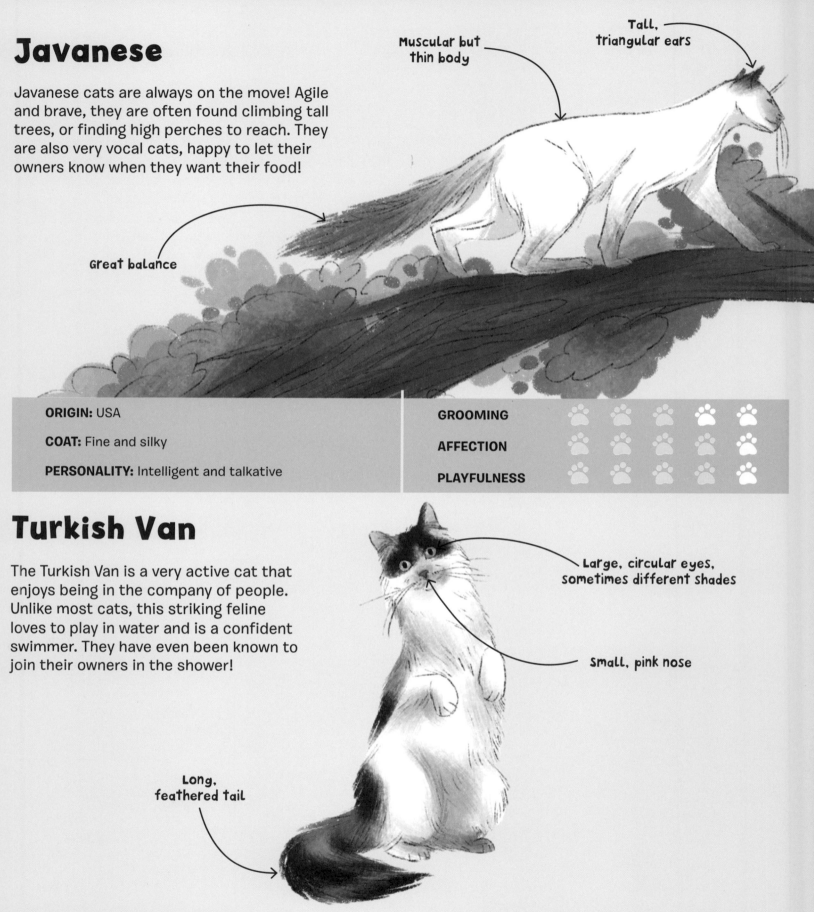

Muscular but thin body

Tall, triangular ears

Great balance

ORIGIN: USA

COAT: Fine and silky

PERSONALITY: Intelligent and talkative

GROOMING

AFFECTION

PLAYFULNESS

Turkish Van

The Turkish Van is a very active cat that enjoys being in the company of people. Unlike most cats, this striking feline loves to play in water and is a confident swimmer. They have even been known to join their owners in the shower!

Large, circular eyes, sometimes different shades

Small, pink nose

Long, feathered tail

ORIGIN: Turkey

COAT: Fine and soft

PERSONALITY: Energetic and fun-loving

GROOMING

AFFECTION

PLAYFULNESS

Turkish Angora

This pretty feline is a very rare breed of cat and is considered a national treasure in its origin country of Turkey. They are very sociable, so they don't like to be alone for long periods of time; if they are, Turkish Angoras are known to get up to mischief!

Eyes are often different shades

Long legs for jumping and playing!

Long, bushy tail

ORIGIN: Turkey

COAT: Glossy and soft

PERSONALITY: Intelligent and friendly

GROOMING 🐾 🐾 🐾

AFFECTION 🐾 🐾 🐾 🐾 🐾

PLAYFULNESS 🐾 🐾 🐾 🐾

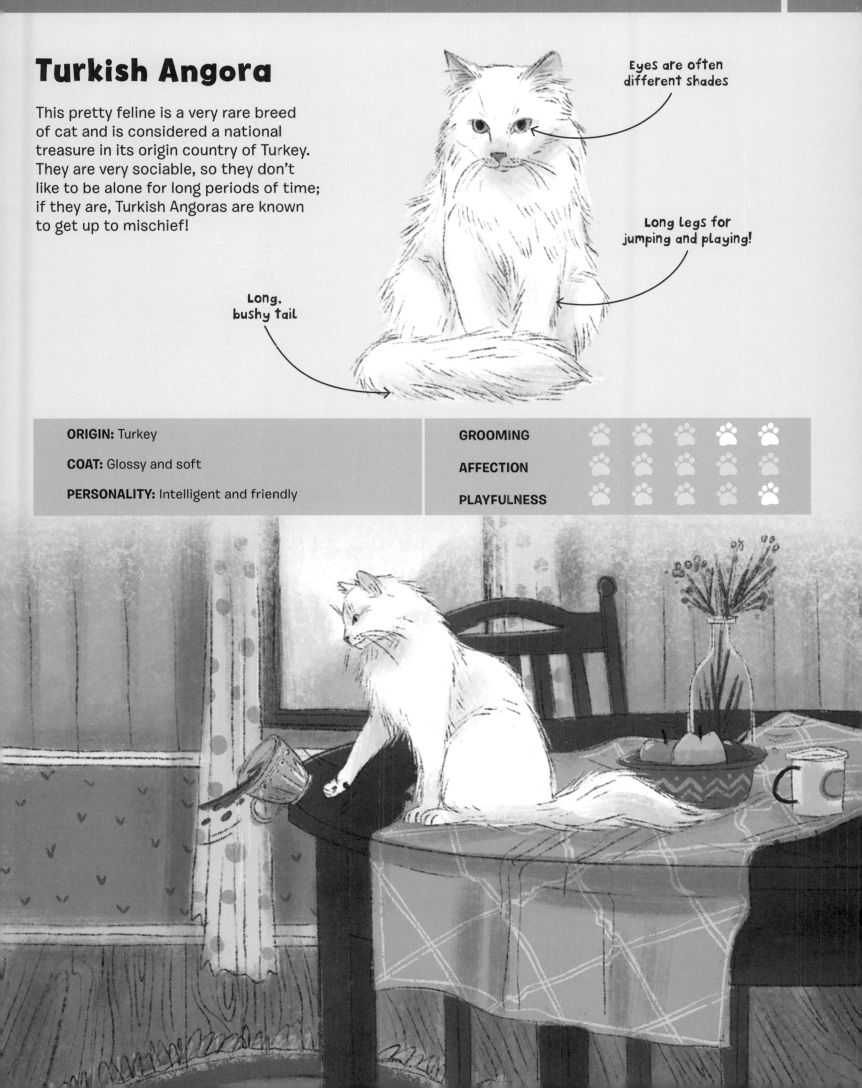

Himalayan

Himalayan cats are a mix of the popular breeds Persian (page 25) and Siamese (page 42), and originated in the early 1900s. This large feline is known for its extremely thick coat and bright, blue eyes. This cat loves a snooze!

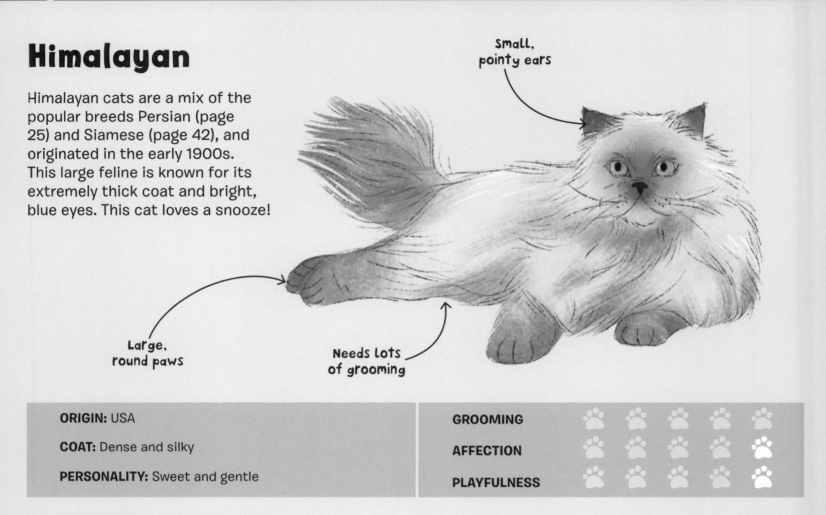

Small, pointy ears

Large, round paws

Needs lots of grooming

ORIGIN: USA	**GROOMING**	🐾🐾🐾🐾🐾
COAT: Dense and silky	**AFFECTION**	🐾🐾🐾🐾🐾
PERSONALITY: Sweet and gentle	**PLAYFULNESS**	🐾🐾🐾🐾🐾

York Chocolate

York chocolate cats are known for their luxuriously soft coats. They are affectionate pets and love to be surrounded by people. As much as these pretty felines love a cuddle on their owner's lap, they are also skilled hunters outdoors too.

Thin neck

Thick, bushy tail

Strong, sturdy legs

ORIGIN: USA	**GROOMING**	🐾🐾🐾🐾🐾
COAT: Thick and soft	**AFFECTION**	🐾🐾🐾🐾🐾
PERSONALITY: Curious and loving	**PLAYFULNESS**	🐾🐾🐾🐾🐾

Nebelung

The Nebelung has a really thick coat, specifically the mane-like fur that surrounds its neck. This handsome breed prefers a quiet **environment** over a busy household and is often found sleeping on the lap of its owner!

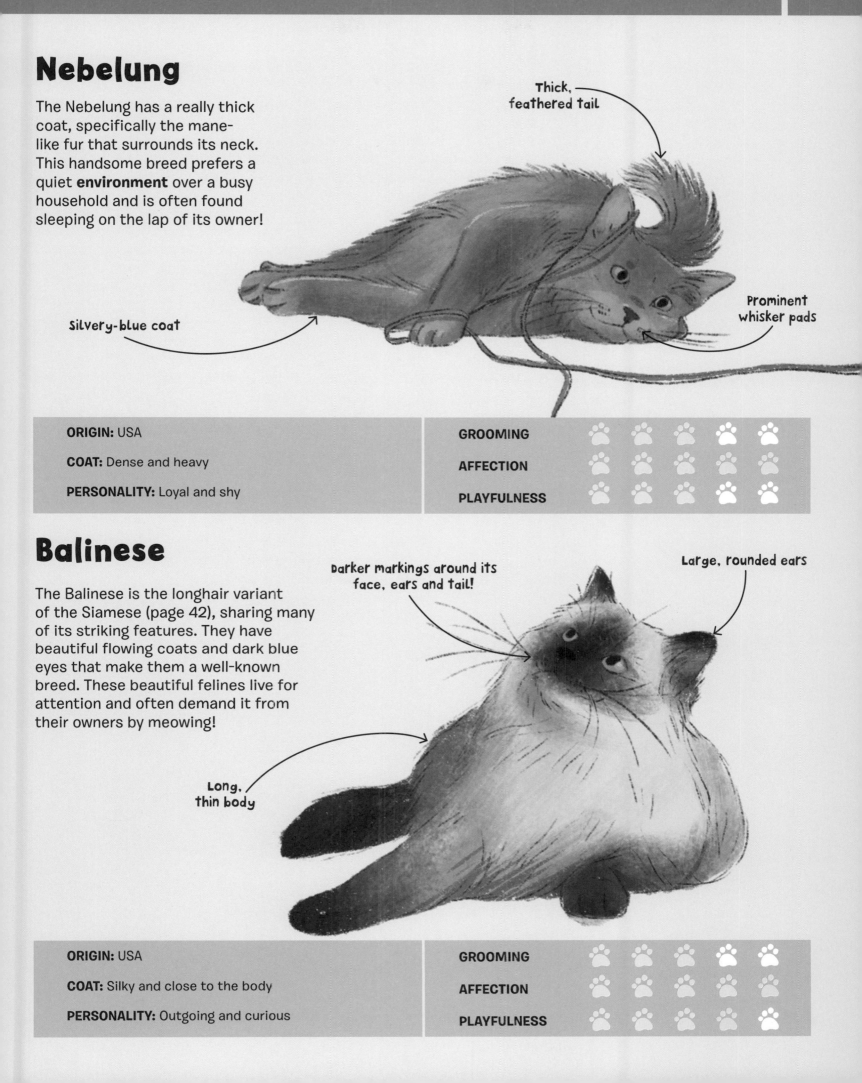

Thick, feathered tail

Prominent whisker pads

Silvery-blue coat

		GROOMING	🐾 🐾 🐾 🐾 🐾
ORIGIN: USA		AFFECTION	🐾 🐾 🐾 🐾 🐾
COAT: Dense and heavy			
PERSONALITY: Loyal and shy		PLAYFULNESS	🐾 🐾 🐾 🐾 🐾

Balinese

The Balinese is the longhair variant of the Siamese (page 42), sharing many of its striking features. They have beautiful flowing coats and dark blue eyes that make them a well-known breed. These beautiful felines live for attention and often demand it from their owners by meowing!

Darker markings around its face, ears and tail!

Large, rounded ears

Long, thin body

	GROOMING	🐾 🐾 🐾 🐾 🐾
ORIGIN: USA		
COAT: Silky and close to the body	AFFECTION	🐾 🐾 🐾 🐾 🐾
PERSONALITY: Outgoing and curious	PLAYFULNESS	🐾 🐾 🐾 🐾 🐾

FUNKY FELINE FEATURES

Ever wondered how big the biggest cat really is?
Or what a cat with no tail might look like? How about a
cat with extremely short legs?

From cats with curly coats to felines without a matching
pair of eyes, these quirky and charming characteristics
make these one-of-a-kind cats stand out from the crowd.
Let's check out the cats with funky feline features!

Maine Coon

The Maine coon is the largest domestic cat breed in the world. This impressive feline is celebrated as the native cat of America. They have a thick, waterproof coat that thickens in colder months and sheds in warmer months. They can be as big as a medium-sized dog!

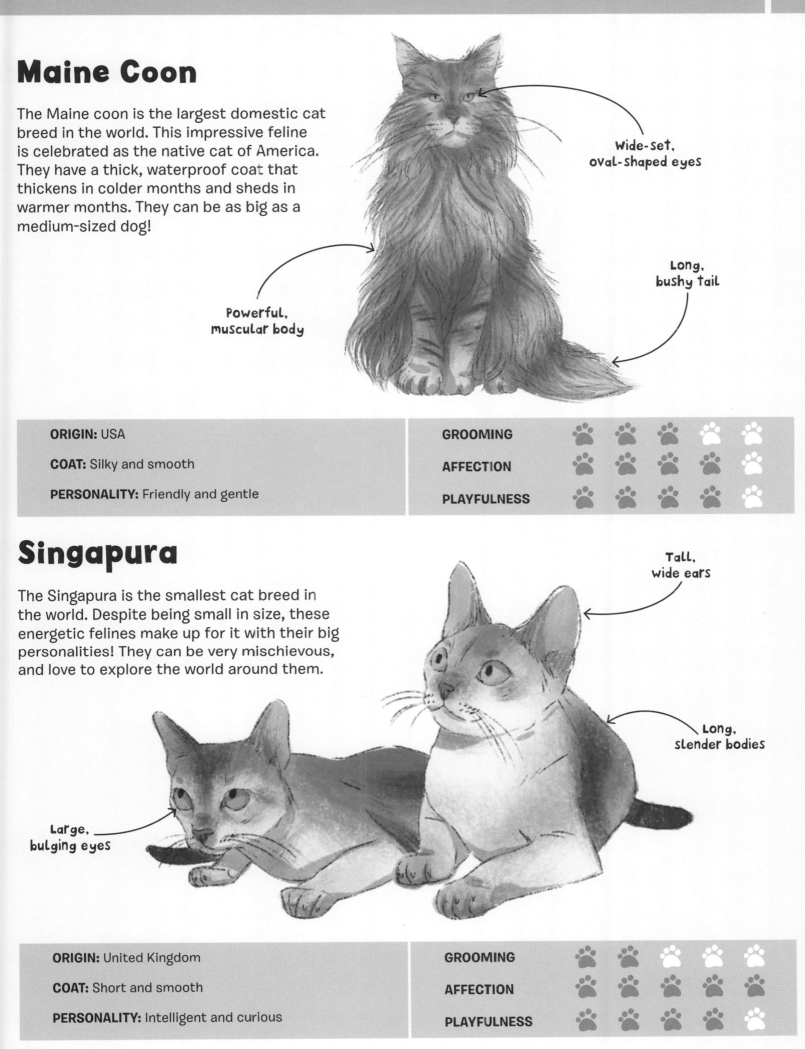

Wide-set, oval-shaped eyes

Long, bushy tail

Powerful, muscular body

ORIGIN: USA

COAT: Silky and smooth

PERSONALITY: Friendly and gentle

GROOMING

AFFECTION

PLAYFULNESS

Singapura

The Singapura is the smallest cat breed in the world. Despite being small in size, these energetic felines make up for it with their big personalities! They can be very mischievous, and love to explore the world around them.

Tall, wide ears

Long, slender bodies

Large, bulging eyes

ORIGIN: United Kingdom

COAT: Short and smooth

PERSONALITY: Intelligent and curious

GROOMING

AFFECTION

PLAYFULNESS

American Wirehair

The American wirehair is best known for its unusual **wiry** coat! The **crimped** fur curls round on itself, making its coat bristly and rough to touch. These cats enjoy playing with their owners but much prefer a quieter indoor space.

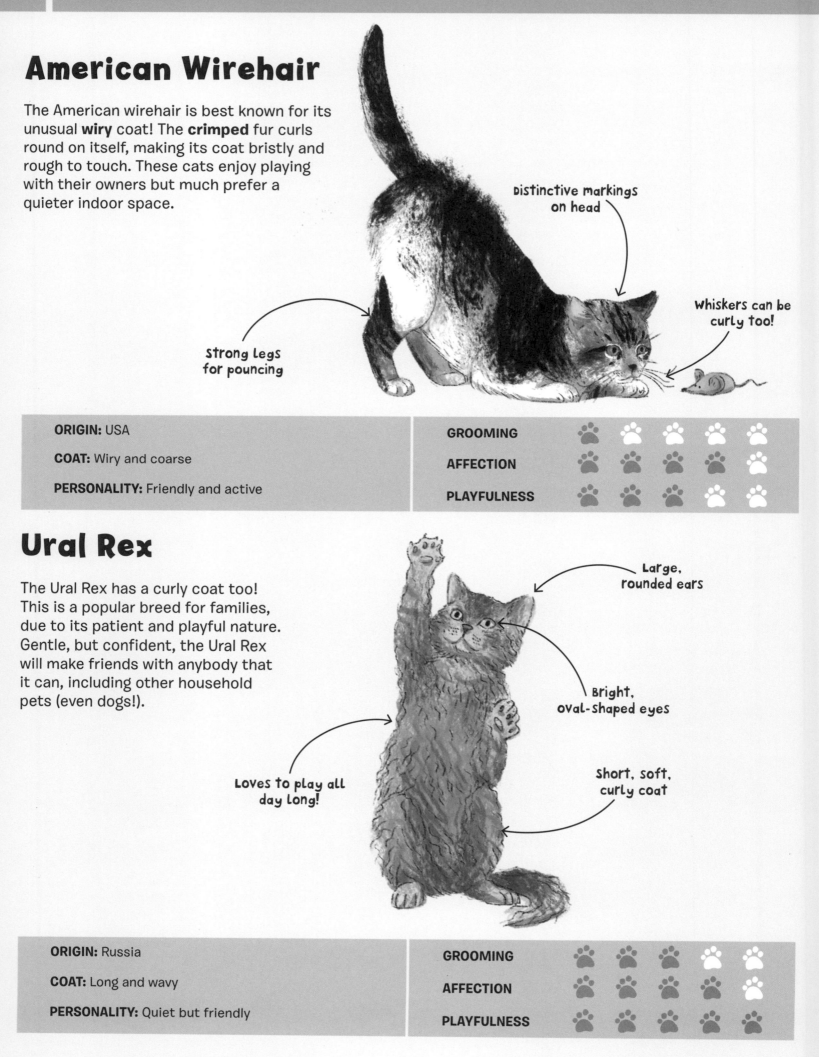

Distinctive markings on head

whiskers can be curly too!

Strong legs for pouncing

ORIGIN: USA	**GROOMING**
COAT: Wiry and coarse	**AFFECTION**
PERSONALITY: Friendly and active	**PLAYFULNESS**

Ural Rex

The Ural Rex has a curly coat too! This is a popular breed for families, due to its patient and playful nature. Gentle, but confident, the Ural Rex will make friends with anybody that it can, including other household pets (even dogs!).

Large, rounded ears

Bright, oval-shaped eyes

Short, soft, curly coat

Loves to play all day long!

ORIGIN: Russia	**GROOMING**
COAT: Long and wavy	**AFFECTION**
PERSONALITY: Quiet but friendly	**PLAYFULNESS**

Sphynx

Sphynx are most well-known for having no fur at all! These hairless felines were named because of how similar they looked to the Egyptian **monument** of the Sphinx. Though their appearance is not appealing to everybody, these cats are very loving and friendly.

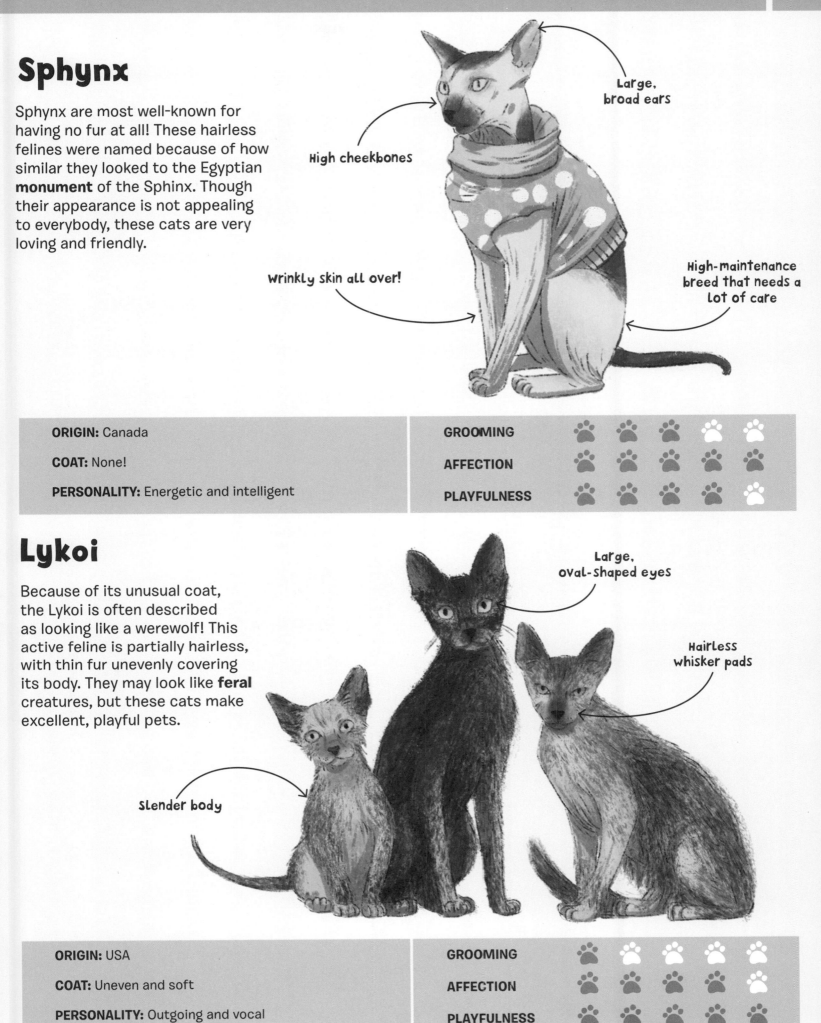

High cheekbones

Large, broad ears

Wrinkly skin all over!

High-maintenance breed that needs a lot of care

ORIGIN: Canada

COAT: None!

PERSONALITY: Energetic and intelligent

GROOMING

AFFECTION

PLAYFULNESS

Lykoi

Because of its unusual coat, the Lykoi is often described as looking like a werewolf! This active feline is partially hairless, with thin fur unevenly covering its body. They may look like **feral** creatures, but these cats make excellent, playful pets.

Large, oval-shaped eyes

Hairless whisker pads

Slender body

ORIGIN: USA

COAT: Uneven and soft

PERSONALITY: Outgoing and vocal

GROOMING

AFFECTION

PLAYFULNESS

Khao Manee

Khao Manees can have blue, yellow or green eyes and sometimes they don't have a matching pair! They are very talkative and will purr or chirp loudly when they are happy. These fascinating felines are loyal to their owners and do not like to be away from them for too long!

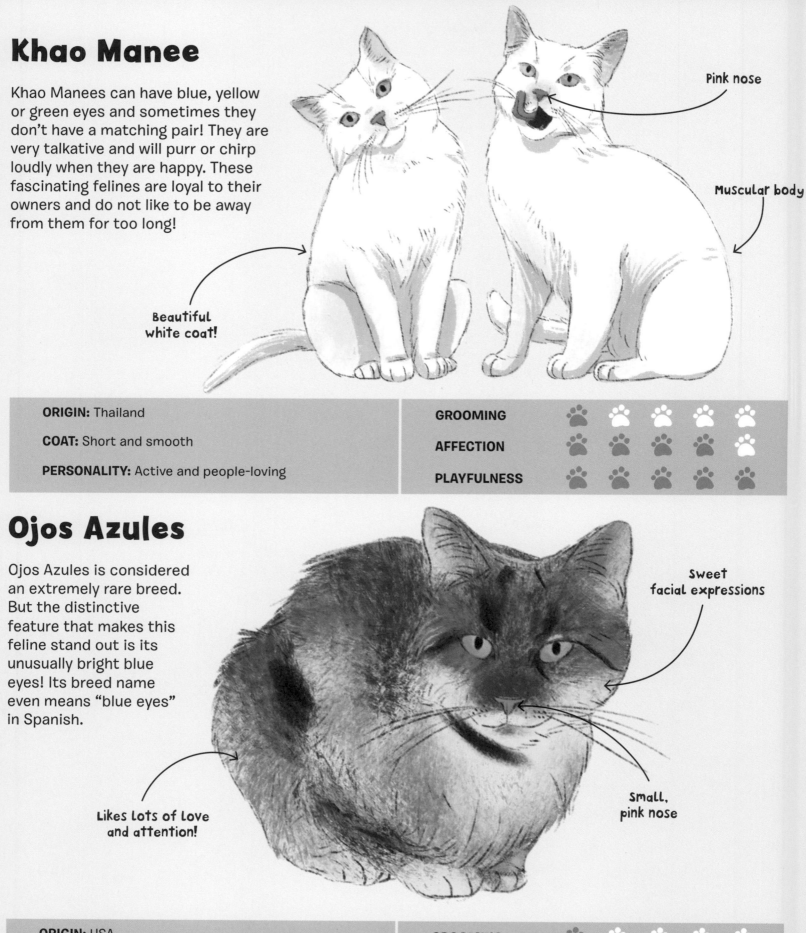

Pink nose

Muscular body

Beautiful white coat!

ORIGIN: Thailand

COAT: Short and smooth

PERSONALITY: Active and people-loving

GROOMING

AFFECTION

PLAYFULNESS

Ojos Azules

Ojos Azules is considered an extremely rare breed. But the distinctive feature that makes this feline stand out is its unusually bright blue eyes! Its breed name even means "blue eyes" in Spanish.

Sweet facial expressions

Small, pink nose

Likes Lots of Love and attention!

ORIGIN: USA

COAT: Short and fine

PERSONALITY: Friendly and gentle

GROOMING

AFFECTION

PLAYFULNESS

Russian Blue

Russian blue cats are easy to spot, as they have beautiful, bluish coats and piercing, green eyes. It takes roughly four months for these felines to develop these bright eyes, sometimes starting off as shades of amber or yellow.

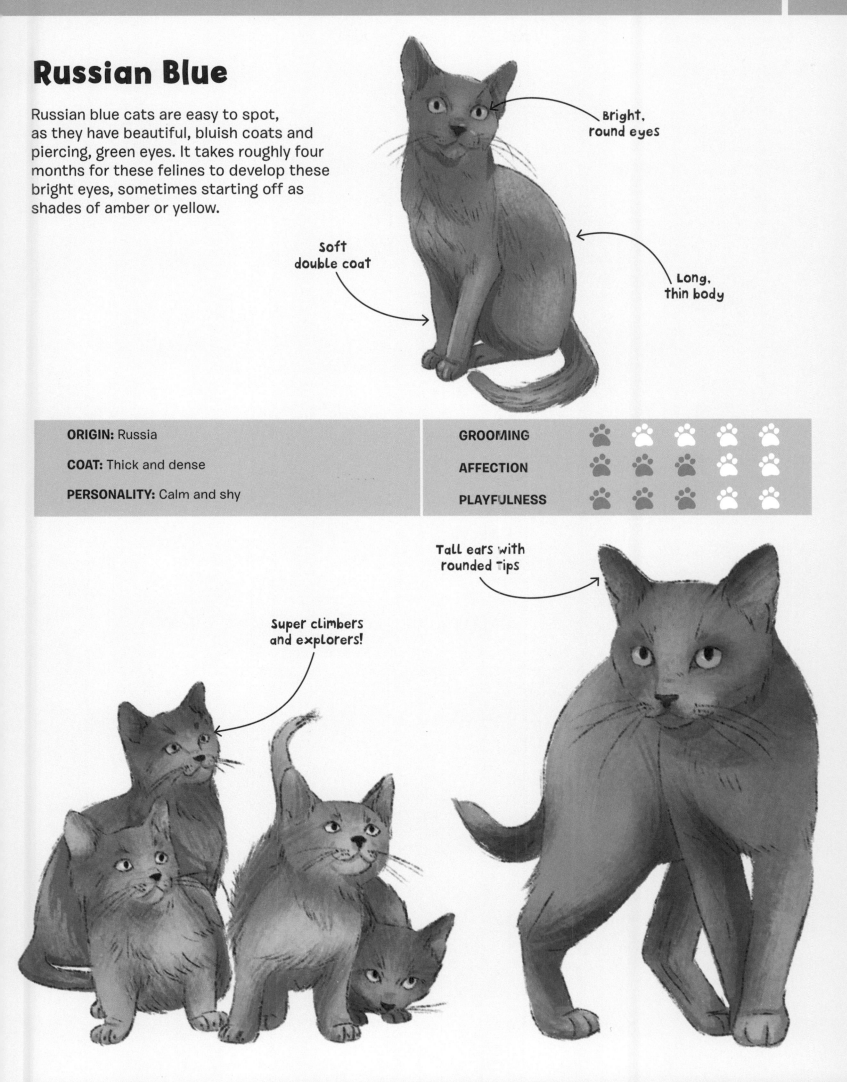

Bright, round eyes

Soft double coat

Long, thin body

ORIGIN: Russia

COAT: Thick and dense

PERSONALITY: Calm and shy

GROOMING

AFFECTION

PLAYFULNESS

Tall ears with rounded tips

Super climbers and explorers!

Siamese

One of the most well-known cat breeds in the world is the Siamese. These elegant felines need lots of playtime, especially outdoors. As well as enjoying calm environments, these curious cats love to climb and explore!

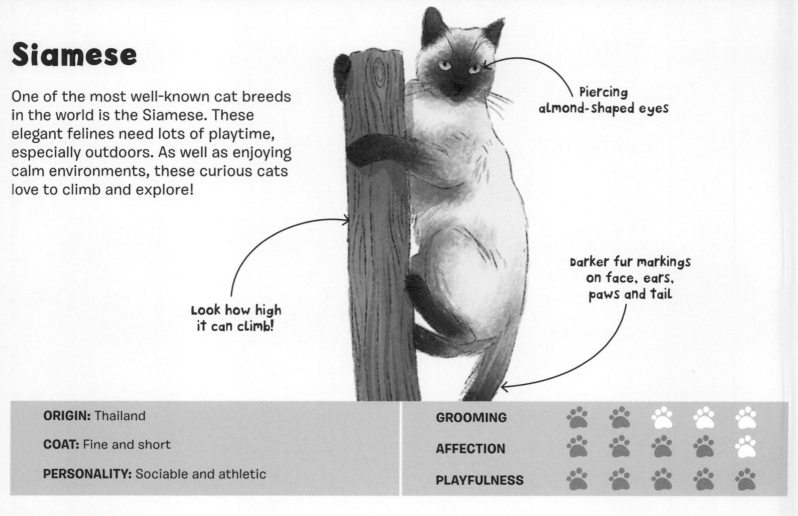

Piercing almond-shaped eyes

Look how high it can climb!

Darker fur markings on face, ears, paws and tail

ORIGIN: Thailand	**GROOMING** 🐾🐾🐾🐾🐾
COAT: Fine and short	**AFFECTION** 🐾🐾🐾🐾🐾
PERSONALITY: Sociable and athletic	**PLAYFULNESS** 🐾🐾🐾🐾🐾

Munchkin

Munchkins have extremely short legs! Despite their small size, these active felines love to play high-energy games with their owners and can run very fast. This unique breed can be either longhair or shorthair cats.

Round, golden eyes

Tail is the same length as its body!

Thick, waterproof coat

ORIGIN: USA	**GROOMING** 🐾🐾🐾🐾🐾
COAT: Smooth and thick	**AFFECTION** 🐾🐾🐾🐾🐾
PERSONALITY: Loyal and energetic	**PLAYFULNESS** 🐾🐾🐾🐾🐾

Chausie

The Chausie was originally believed to have developed from a mix of wildcat and domestic cat, giving it its untamed appearance. This striking feline requires lots of company and attention from its owners, and is known to get along well with dogs!

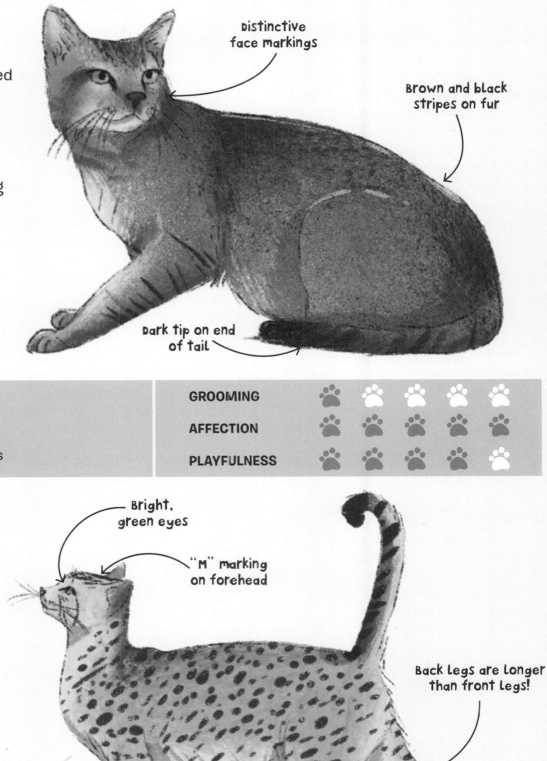

distinctive face markings

Brown and black stripes on fur

Dark tip on end of tail

ORIGIN: USA

COAT: Short and silky

PERSONALITY: Active and curious

GROOMING

AFFECTION

PLAYFULNESS

Egyptian Mau

The Egyptian Mau is one of the only domesticated cats that has a naturally spotted coat. This majestic breed dates back to ancient Egypt, and can be seen in many **tomb** paintings from the time. Although they can be very loving toward their owners, they're very shy and cautious around anybody else!

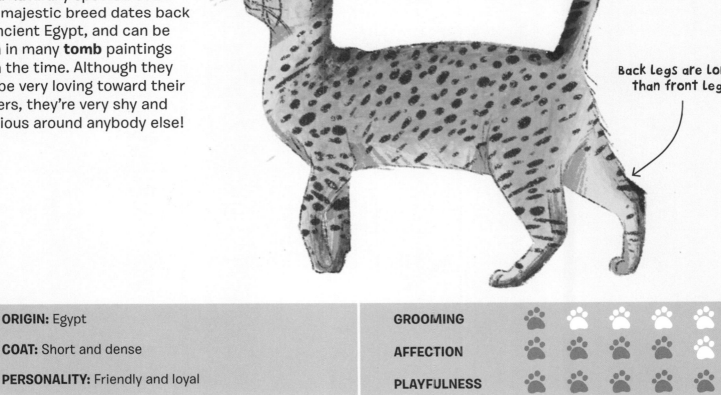

Bright, green eyes

"M" marking on forehead

Back legs are longer than front legs!

ORIGIN: Egypt

COAT: Short and dense

PERSONALITY: Friendly and loyal

GROOMING

AFFECTION

PLAYFULNESS

Japanese Bobtail

The Japanese bobtail is easy to spot because of its small, round tail that looks just like the tail of a rabbit. This breed originated in Japan and is believed to bring good luck. This sweet feline would be happy playing with its owners all day long!

Round, golden eyes

Thin but muscular body

Back legs are much longer than front legs!

ORIGIN: Japan

COAT: Silky and soft

PERSONALITY: Intelligent and outgoing

GROOMING	🐾	🐾	🐾	🐾	🐾
AFFECTION	🐾	🐾	🐾	🐾	🐾
PLAYFULNESS	🐾	🐾	🐾	🐾	🐾

American Ringtail

Like its name suggests, the American ringtail is easily spotted by its tail that is twisted into the shape of a ring. This unique-looking feline is the only cat breed to have a tail like this. They are curious cats, with a particular love for climbing.

Athletic build

This is a very noisy cat!

Long, powerful legs

ORIGIN: USA

COAT: Silky and soft

PERSONALITY: Active and vocal

GROOMING	🐾	🐾	🐾	🐾	🐾
AFFECTION	🐾	🐾	🐾	🐾	🐾
PLAYFULNESS	🐾	🐾	🐾	🐾	🐾

Pixiebob

The Pixiebob gets its name from its extremely short tail. Despite looking like its wildcat relative, the bobcat (page 58), this feline is known for its sweet, gentle nature and love of being around people. They are also described as having dog-like personalities because they enjoy playing in water!

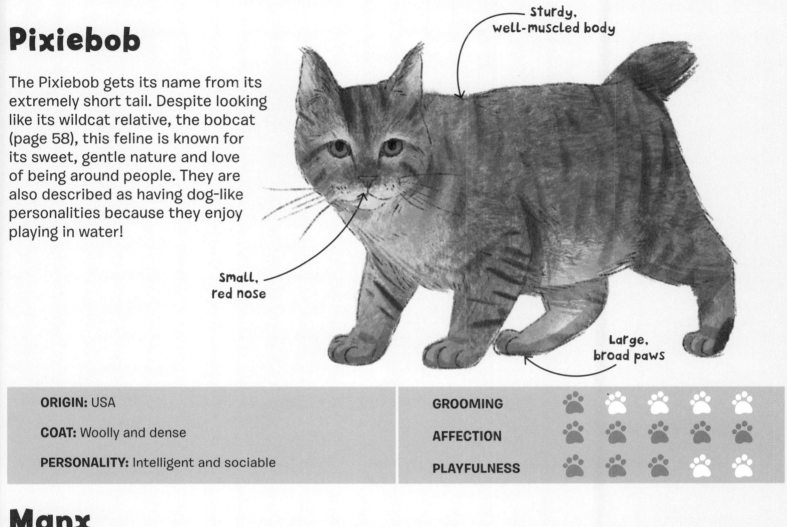

Sturdy, well-muscled body

Small, red nose

Large, broad paws

ORIGIN: USA	
COAT: Woolly and dense	
PERSONALITY: Intelligent and sociable	

GROOMING 🐾 🐾 🐾 🐾 🐾

AFFECTION 🐾 🐾 🐾 🐾 🐾

PLAYFULNESS 🐾 🐾 🐾 🐾 🐾

Manx

Manx cats have no tail at all! Instead, the end of their small bodies have a short stump where the tail should be. This unusual breed is popular with cat owners for its unique appearance and sweet nature. They are very curious cats, playing with anything they find!

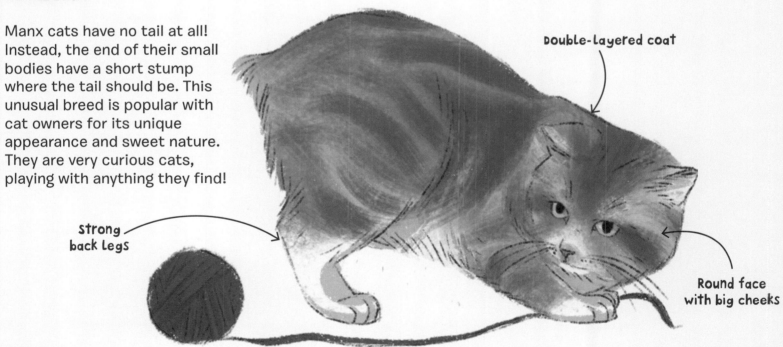

Double-layered coat

Round face with big cheeks

Strong back legs

ORIGIN: United Kingdom	
COAT: Thick and dense	
PERSONALITY: Gentle and calm	

GROOMING 🐾 🐾 🐾 🐾 🐾

AFFECTION 🐾 🐾 🐾 🐾 🐾

PLAYFULNESS 🐾 🐾 🐾 🐾 🐾

Scottish Fold

Scottish folds are best known for having large, golden eyes and folded over ears! Their unique ears bend forward and lay flat against their head. These cats are known for being very loyal creatures, and love quality time with their owners.

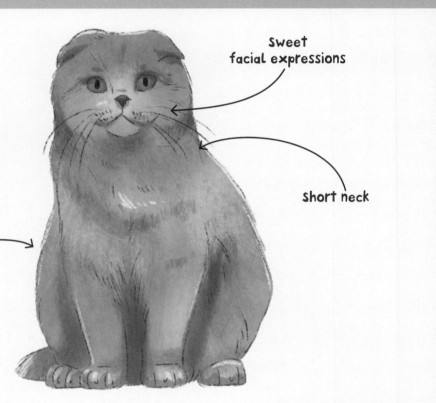

Sweet facial expressions

Short neck

Rounded, solid body

ORIGIN: Scotland	GROOMING	🐾🐾🐾🐾🐾
COAT: Short and dense	AFFECTION	🐾🐾🐾🐾🐾
PERSONALITY: Quiet and friendly	PLAYFULNESS	🐾🐾🐾🐾🐾

American Curl

Similar to the Highlander (page 47), the American curl, as its name suggests, has ears that curl far back on the top of its head. Sociable and nosy, American curls love to be involved in their owners' lives, "helping" them as much as possible!

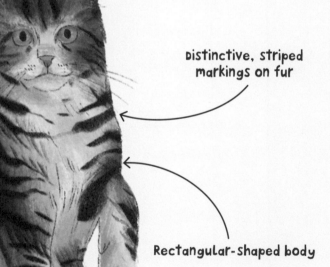

Distinctive, striped markings on fur

Thick, bushy tail

Rectangular-shaped body

ORIGIN: USA	GROOMING	🐾🐾🐾🐾🐾
COAT: Soft and silky	AFFECTION	🐾🐾🐾🐾🐾
PERSONALITY: Loving and engaging	PLAYFULNESS	🐾🐾🐾🐾🐾

Highlander

The Highlander is a fairly new breed of cat and is best known for ears that bend backward. These energetic cats are always in the mood to play! They are loyal to their owners, and can be either shorthair or longhair cats.

stripy or spotty fur, and sometimes has both!

Well-built, strong body

Large, round paws

ORIGIN: USA	
COAT: Soft and thick	
PERSONALITY: Active and loving	

GROOMING	🐾 🐾
AFFECTION	🐾 🐾 🐾 🐾
PLAYFULNESS	🐾 🐾 🐾 🐾 🐾

can play all day long

Has a short tail that wags when it's happy!

CUNNING WILD CATS

From the little oncilla that spends its days pouncing on **prey** from trees to the powerful lion that lazes by day and hunts at night, there are so many wild cats to explore. They live in lots of different habitats all around the world.

These types of cats live in the wild outdoors and do not rely on humans to survive. They are independent, deadly creatures that can't and shouldn't be tamed! It's time to delve into the world of cunning wild cats...

Cheetah

The cheetah is not only the fastest cat, but the fastest animal in the world too! These speedy wild cats have golden fur and are covered in black spots. They might not pose a threat to humans, but you should stay far back when they're chasing prey!

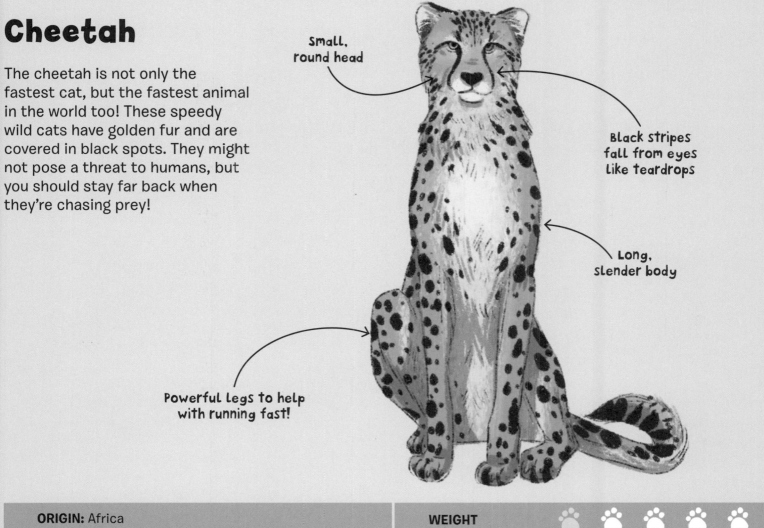

Small, round head

Black stripes fall from eyes like teardrops

Long, slender body

Powerful legs to help with running fast!

ORIGIN: Africa	
COAT: Short and rough	
PERSONALITY: Gentle and shy	

WEIGHT	🐾 🐾 🐾 🐾 🐾
SPEED	🐾 🐾 🐾 🐾 🐾
ENDANGERED STATUS	🐾 🐾 🐾 🐾 🐾

Tiger

The tiger is the largest species of cat in the world! These strong big cats are easy to identify by their orange coats covered in bold, black stripes. They tend to live alone and, unlike most cats, love swimming in water.

Spotty, round ears

Long whiskers

Large, padded feet

ORIGIN: Asia	
COAT: Thick and coarse	
PERSONALITY: Independent and fierce	

WEIGHT	🐾	🐾	🐾	🐾	🐾
SPEED	🐾	🐾	🐾	🐾	🐾
ENDANGERED STATUS	🐾	🐾	🐾	🐾	🐾

Mountain Lion (Puma)

Mountain lions are known by many names, including puma, panther and cougar. These secretive wild cats are one of the largest carnivores in America, and are very hard to spot. They are very **adaptable** so can live in lots of different environments!

Large, muscular body

Sharp, curved claws

Light brown fur

ORIGIN: USA	
COAT: Thick and soft	
PERSONALITY: Solitary and **nocturnal**	

WEIGHT	🐾	🐾	🐾	🐾	🐾
SPEED	🐾	🐾	🐾	🐾	🐾
ENDANGERED STATUS	🐾	🐾	🐾	🐾	🐾

Lion

Lions are best known for their large manes and their powerful roar! They live in groups called prides and the males are nicknamed the "king of the jungle". These big cats may be deadly hunters but they often spend most of the day sleeping!

Large, round head

only males have shaggy manes!

strong, muscular body

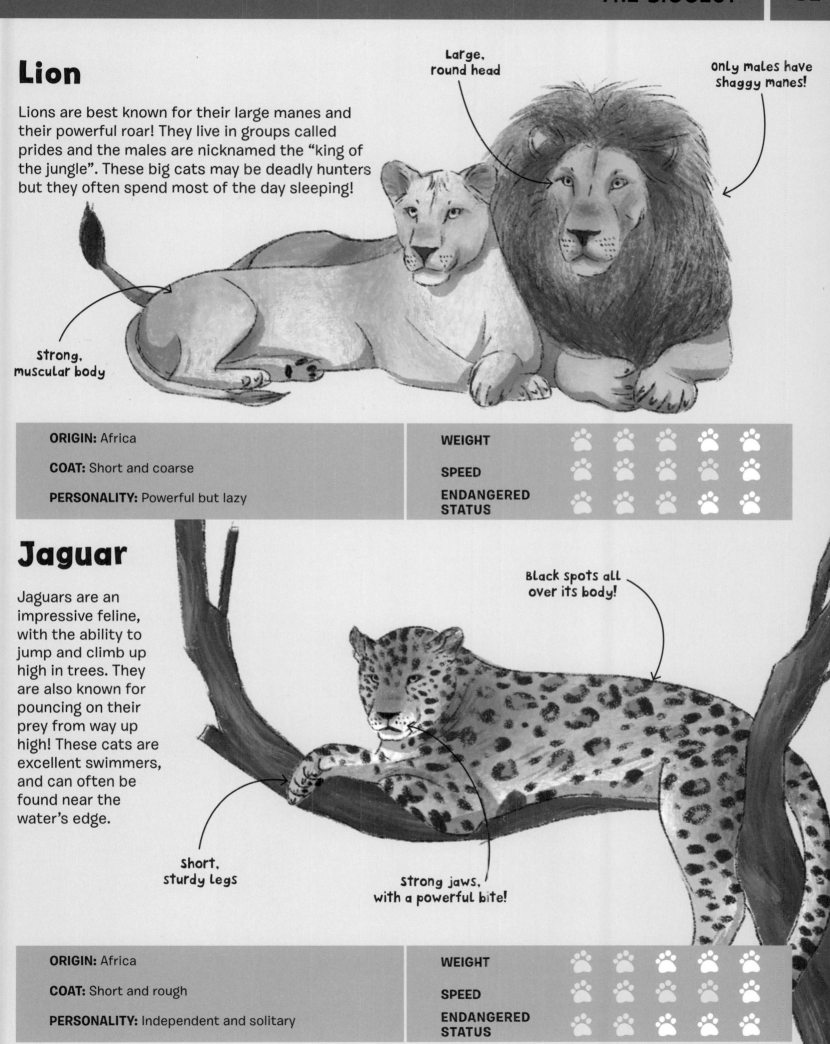

ORIGIN: Africa	WEIGHT	🐾 🐾 🐾 🐾 🐾
COAT: Short and coarse	SPEED	🐾 🐾 🐾 🐾 🐾
PERSONALITY: Powerful but lazy	ENDANGERED STATUS	🐾 🐾 🐾 🐾 🐾

Jaguar

Jaguars are an impressive feline, with the ability to jump and climb up high in trees. They are also known for pouncing on their prey from way up high! These cats are excellent swimmers, and can often be found near the water's edge.

Black spots all over its body!

Short, sturdy legs

strong jaws, with a powerful bite!

ORIGIN: Africa	WEIGHT	🐾 🐾 🐾 🐾 🐾
COAT: Short and rough	SPEED	🐾 🐾 🐾 🐾 🐾
PERSONALITY: Independent and solitary	ENDANGERED STATUS	🐾 🐾 🐾 🐾 🐾

Black-Footed Cat (Small-Spotted Cat)

The black-footed cat is considered the deadliest cat in the world. Despite being the smallest species of wild cat in Africa, this solitary cat searches for prey during the night and has a high success rate when it hunts!

Its eyesight is six times better than humans!

Under its coat, it has pink skin!

Dark spots on light fur

ORIGIN: South Africa

COAT: Soft and dense

PERSONALITY: Bold and independent

WEIGHT

SPEED

ENDANGERED STATUS

Rusty-Spotted Cat

Rusty-spotted cats are one of the smallest cat species in the world, only weighing up to 4 pounds (2 kg). Despite being small, this cat is known to hunt small **mammals** that are the same size as themselves! These tiny cats are very secretive, so little is known about how they behave.

Dark brown spots across body

Large, round eyes

Long, thick tail that is darker than the rest of the body

ORIGIN: India

COAT: Short and soft

PERSONALITY: Nocturnal and active

WEIGHT

SPEED

ENDANGERED STATUS

Kodkod

Kodkods are the smallest wild cat in America and are closely related to the margay (page 57). They tend to live in rainforests and coastal forests. This shy feline spends lots of its time awake, resting in the day and then exploring and hunting at night.

They are usually brown and spotty, but can have black coats too!

Long, slender body

Black spots all over fur, even if you can't see them!

ORIGIN: Chile	WEIGHT	🐾 🐾 🐾 🐾 🐾
COAT: Thick and dense	SPEED	🐾 🐾 🐾 🐾 🐾
PERSONALITY: Secretive and solitary	ENDANGERED STATUS	🐾 🐾 🐾 🐾 🐾

Oncilla

Oncilla are one of the smallest wild cats in South America, hunting at night and choosing to live a solitary life. This feisty wild cat will hide in trees and look for its prey down below, waiting for the perfect opportunity to pounce!

Eyes vary from light to dark brown

Dark brown spots, outlined by black circles

Fantastic climber!

ORIGIN: Central and South America	WEIGHT	🐾 🐾 🐾 🐾 🐾
COAT: Short and thick	SPEED	🐾 🐾 🐾 🐾 🐾
PERSONALITY: Aggressive and independent	ENDANGERED STATUS	🐾 🐾 🐾 🐾 🐾

Leopard

Similar to a jaguar (page 51) in appearance, the leopard is a skilled hunter that only comes out at night. These powerful felines are great climbers, and are able to pull their prey high up into the trees! They eat all sorts of prey, from little bugs to big antelopes.

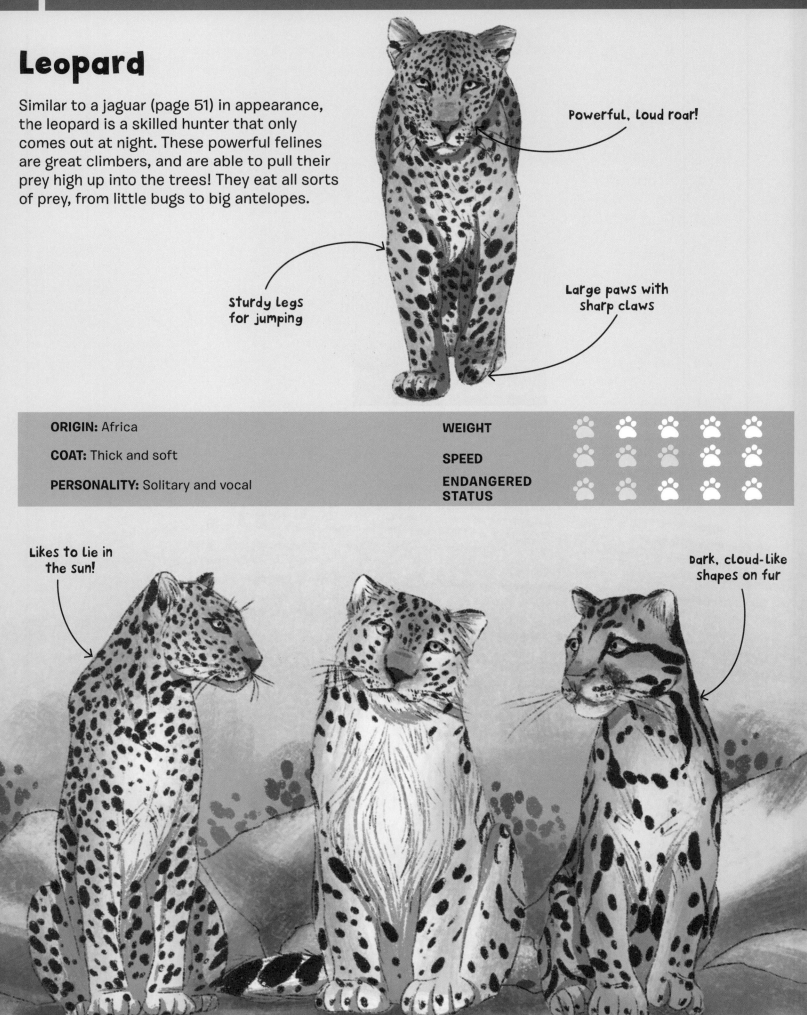

Powerful, loud roar!

Sturdy legs for jumping

Large paws with sharp claws

ORIGIN: Africa

COAT: Thick and soft

PERSONALITY: Solitary and vocal

WEIGHT

SPEED

ENDANGERED STATUS

Likes to lie in the sun!

Dark, cloud-like shapes on fur

Clouded Leopard

The clouded leopard is one of the oldest species of cat in the world. This little wild cat is a very clever and quiet **predator**, and can't roar or purr. They are very rarely seen by humans, so little is known about this secretive wild cat.

Long, slender body

Extremely long tail!

Has special pads on its feet to help grip to branches

ORIGIN: Asia	WEIGHT	🐾 🐾 🐾 🐾 🐾
COAT: Soft and dense	SPEED	🐾 🐾 🐾 🐾 🐾
PERSONALITY: Nocturnal and solitary	ENDANGERED STATUS	🐾 🐾 🐾 🐾 🐾

Snow Leopard

Snow leopards are experts at **camouflage**! They have beautiful thick fur that blends in with their snowy habitat, keeping them hidden from unsuspecting prey. They have large paws covered in thick fur that keep them warm against the snow.

Well adapted to the cold weather!

Long, bushy tail

Strong, powerful legs for jumping

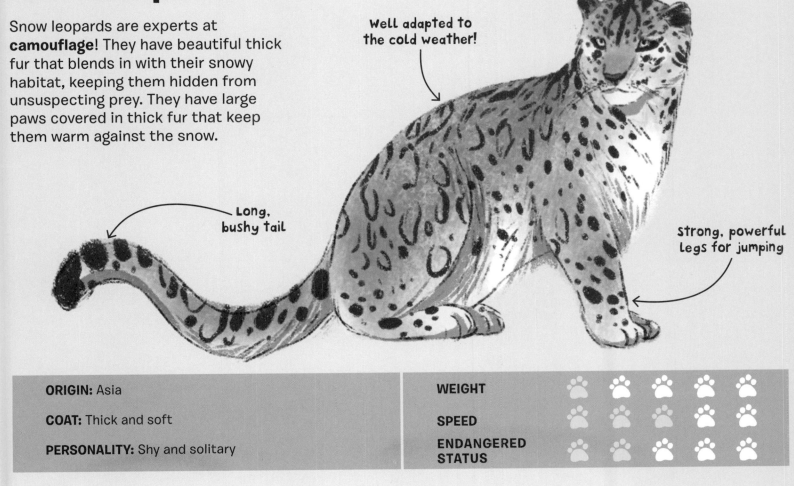

ORIGIN: Asia	WEIGHT	🐾 🐾 🐾 🐾 🐾
COAT: Thick and soft	SPEED	🐾 🐾 🐾 🐾 🐾
PERSONALITY: Shy and solitary	ENDANGERED STATUS	🐾 🐾 🐾 🐾 🐾

Serval

Servals have very large, tall ears and look like a small version of a cheetah (page 49)! They are active cats that jump high to catch birds above and dig deep into the ground to find prey below. Despite their small size, these clever felines can reach speeds of 45 mph (72 km/h).

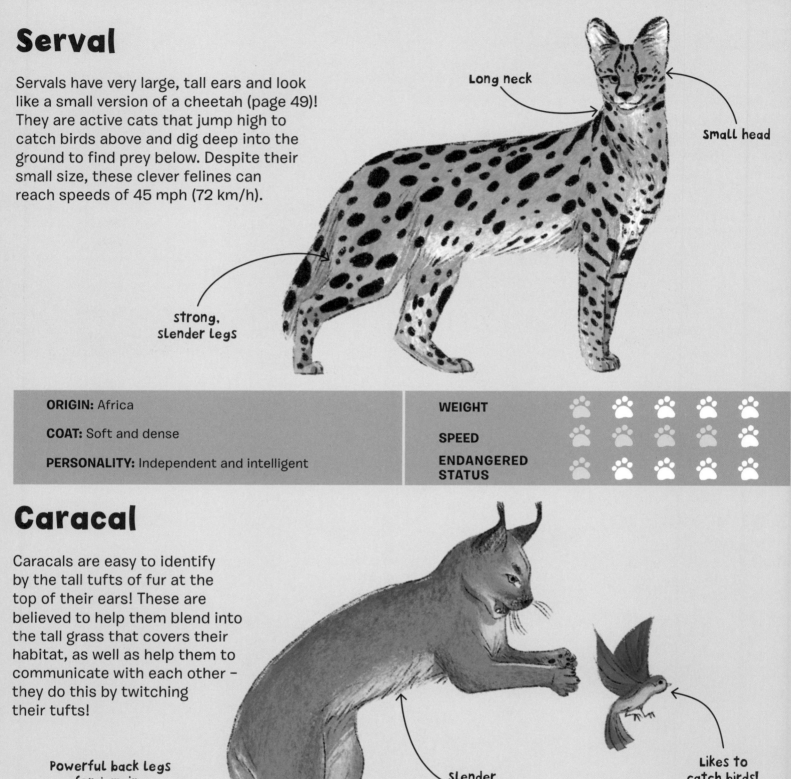

Long neck

Small head

strong, slender legs

ORIGIN: Africa	**WEIGHT**	🐾 🐾 🐾 🐾 🐾
COAT: Soft and dense	**SPEED**	🐾 🐾 🐾 🐾 🐾
PERSONALITY: Independent and intelligent	**ENDANGERED STATUS**	🐾 🐾 🐾 🐾 🐾

Caracal

Caracals are easy to identify by the tall tufts of fur at the top of their ears! These are believed to help them blend into the tall grass that covers their habitat, as well as help them to communicate with each other – they do this by twitching their tufts!

Powerful back legs for jumping

Slender, sturdy body

Likes to catch birds!

ORIGIN: Africa	**WEIGHT**	🐾 🐾 🐾 🐾 🐾
COAT: Short and soft	**SPEED**	🐾 🐾 🐾 🐾 🐾
PERSONALITY: Secretive and intelligent	**ENDANGERED STATUS**	🐾 🐾 🐾 🐾 🐾

Margay

Margay have unique abilities – they can rotate their ankles 180 degrees. This makes them excellent climbers, and means these flexible felines can climb down trees headfirst. The margay is the monkey of the cat world!

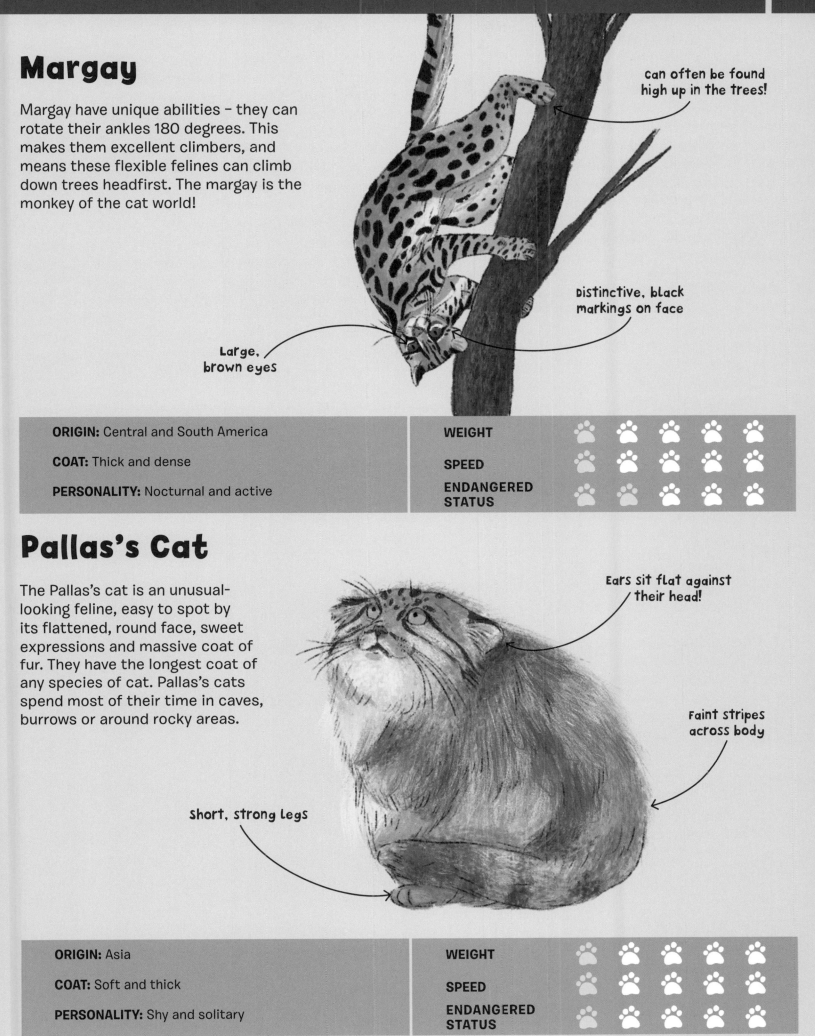

can often be found high up in the trees!

Distinctive, black markings on face

Large, brown eyes

ORIGIN: Central and South America	**WEIGHT** 🐾🐾🐾🐾🐾
COAT: Thick and dense	**SPEED** 🐾🐾🐾🐾🐾
PERSONALITY: Nocturnal and active	**ENDANGERED STATUS** 🐾🐾🐾🐾🐾

Pallas's Cat

The Pallas's cat is an unusual-looking feline, easy to spot by its flattened, round face, sweet expressions and massive coat of fur. They have the longest coat of any species of cat. Pallas's cats spend most of their time in caves, burrows or around rocky areas.

Ears sit flat against their head!

Faint stripes across body

Short, strong legs

ORIGIN: Asia	**WEIGHT** 🐾🐾🐾🐾🐾
COAT: Soft and thick	**SPEED** 🐾🐾🐾🐾🐾
PERSONALITY: Shy and solitary	**ENDANGERED STATUS** 🐾🐾🐾🐾🐾

Lynx

Lynx are small wild cats that live in thick woodlands and rocky mountains. The tufts on their ears are believed to help them hear better, and their fur thickens in the winter to keep them warm. They are independent cats, perfectly built for the cold weather!

Black tufts on the top of the ears!

Lightly spotted fur

Large, **webbed** paws to stop them from slipping

ORIGIN: Europe and Africa	**WEIGHT** 🐾🐾🐾🐾🐾
COAT: Soft and thick	**SPEED** 🐾🐾🐾🐾🐾
PERSONALITY: Reserved and solitary	**ENDANGERED STATUS** 🐾🐾🐾🐾🐾

Bobcat

The bobcat is best known for its short bobble tail! These adaptable felines are capable of living in a wide variety of habitats; from forests and deserts, to coastal areas and scrubland, there is nowhere these cats won't go!

Small, pointy ears

Distinctive markings on face

Black stripes or spots on legs

ORIGIN: North America	**WEIGHT** 🐾🐾🐾🐾🐾
COAT: Short and dense	**SPEED** 🐾🐾🐾🐾🐾
PERSONALITY: Independent and fierce	**ENDANGERED STATUS** 🐾🐾🐾🐾🐾

Flat-Headed Cat

As the name suggests, this striking feline is easy to distinguish by its flat head, as well as its constantly shocked expression! This cat is never too far away from water, choosing to live by marshes, streams, lakes, wetlands, and in rainforests.

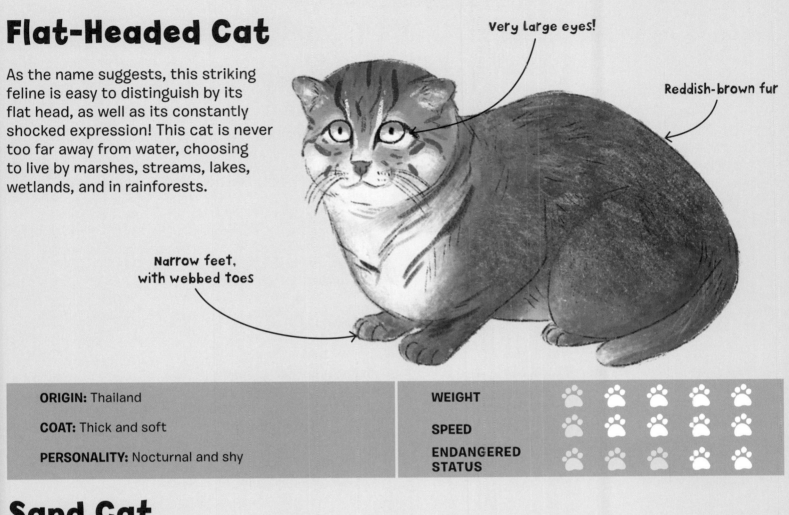

Very large eyes!

Reddish-brown fur

Narrow feet, with webbed toes

ORIGIN: Thailand	**WEIGHT**
COAT: Thick and soft	**SPEED**
PERSONALITY: Nocturnal and shy	**ENDANGERED STATUS**

Sand Cat

The sand cat is well adapted to sweltering climates, living in deserts across Africa and Asia. Their pale fur allows these cute felines to blend in with their environment. These impressive cats can go weeks without drinking any water!

Dark fur markings, from eyes across face

Brown stripes on legs and tail

Sharp claws

ORIGIN: Africa	**WEIGHT**
COAT: Soft and dense	**SPEED**
PERSONALITY: Solitary and vocal	**ENDANGERED STATUS**

GLOSSARY

Adaptable - being able to adjust to new surroundings.

Camouflage - when animals are able to blend in with their surroundings.

Crimped - fur that has small ridges or folds in it.

Crossbreeding – when two cats of different breeds have kittens.

Descendants – people or animals that are related to an individual or group who lived in the past. For example, you are a descendant of your parents and grandparents.

Domestic – an animal that has been tamed or trained to live or work with humans.

Endangered - when a species of any kind is at risk of no longer existing.

Environment - another word for surroundings.

Feral - wild, not domesticated (see above).

Habitat - the natural environment where animals, plants and any other things live.

Mammals - warm-blooded animals that give birth to live young and feed their babies with milk.

Monument - a statue or building made in memory of a person or event.

Nocturnal - an animal that sleeps during the day and becomes active during the night.

Predator - an animal that hunts and kills other animals for food.

Prey - animals that are hunted and killed for food.

Rehoming shelter - a place where cats (or other animals) who were lost, stray or given up by their owners are looked after until they can be adopted into a new home.

Slender - something that is thin and narrow.

Solitary - something that lives alone.

Tomb - a large, underground space for burying and remembering the dead.

Unique - something that stands out and is completely different from everything else.

Webbed - toes that are connected by a thin piece of skin. Some animals have these to help them swim.

Wiry - a type of coat that is rough, thick and bristly.

INDEX

ABOUT THE AUTHOR

Eliza Jeffery is a children's book author based in Falmouth. She is passionate about helping children explore and enjoy the big world around them. She loves exploring Cornwall, and can often be found reading a book and eating a bowl of mussels by the sea!

ABOUT THE ILLUSTRATOR

Marina Halak is a talented illustrator of children's books from Ukraine. Her stunning illustrations are inspired by her own childhood, children, nature, magical moments and fairy tales. Marina is also the illustrator behind the first book in the series, *Dogs*.

PICTURE CREDITS

Shutterstock: Anna Mente 10ml; Creative Cat Studio 11tl; RJ22 10mr.

Every effort has been made to trace the copyright holders, and we apologize in advance for any unintentional omissions. We would be pleased to insert the appropriate acknowledgments in any subsequent edition of this publication.